The ROGERS LOCOMOTIVE
CATALOG, 1876

Published with Funds from

Friends of the Society,

the Estate of Edward J. Grassmann,

and an

Anonymous Gift

Dedicated to the Memory of

Delia Brinckerhoff Koster

The ROGERS LOCOMOTIVE CATALOG, 1876

Introduction by
JOHN H. WHITE, *Jr.*

New Jersey Historical Society

The Rogers Locomotive Catalog, 1876 is a facsimile reproduction of *Locomotives and Locomotive Building, Being a Brief Sketch of Various Improvements in Locomotive Building during the Last Century, together with a History of the Origin and Growth of the Rogers Locomotive and Machine Works, Paterson, New Jersey, from 1831 to 1876* (New York: J. W. Pratt, Printer, 1876). The original copy is in the collections of the New Jersey Historical Society.

INTRODUCTION

Paterson, new jersey, was one of the principal centers of American industry in the nineteenth century. It was best known as home of several major locomotive manufacturers and capital of the American silk industry. Paterson was founded in 1791 as the country's first planned industrial community. Its creation was a direct result of Alexander Hamilton's most enduring dream: a self-sufficient America whose home industry, encouraged by a business-minded society, could make the country economically independent of Great Britain. The city was well situated as the New World's home for "Vulcan." It was only eighteen miles from New York, with access to that city's enormous capital and shipping resources, and possessed a natural power source in the Great Falls of the Passaic River. Heavy industry flourished here for several generations, and for many years Paterson-built locomotives enjoyed an international reputation for their number and excellence. Between 1837 and 1926 almost ten thousand railway engines were produced by Paterson's locomotive manufacturers, including Rogers, Grant, Cooke, and their several predecessor firms. The majority were produced at the Rogers plant, which was the nation's largest locomotive plant between 1850 and 1860, as measured by the total number of engines produced. During this decade Rogers was also the unchallenged leader in the area of technical innovation. The wagon-top boiler, spread trucks, level cylinders, and Stephenson valve were promoted, if not invented, by Rogers.

This leading position began to fade after the 1870s, despite the construction of new shops and tools. The death of William S. Hudson

(1810–81), the firm's long-time mechanical chief, was one set back. Another was the declining interest of Jacob S. Rogers, son of the company's founder, Thomas Rogers. Jacob S. Rogers spent more time away from the shop, and when he resigned in 1893, the firm had slipped to fourth place among American locomotive manufacturers. Meanwhile, industrial giants like Baldwin and the American Locomotive Company came to dominate the field. Small independents like Rogers, with old-fashioned plants, were doomed. The American Locomotive Company purchased Rogers in 1905 and ended production eight years later.

It is not entirely clear why the 1876 Rogers locomotive catalog was published or why it had to be an elaborate hardback book. It would have been relatively expensive to produce in the 1870s. Line engravings were the common form of book illustration at the time, but the 1876 Rogers locomotive catalog reproduced twenty-three locomotives as collotypes (printed by this novel process and probably more expensive than line engravings). The catalog was published in the midst of a terrible economic crisis that began three years before. Locomotives have never been consumer items, and so one wonders if the book was intended only for locomotive superintendents, purchasing agents, and other railroad officials. Perhaps its potential sales value was justification enough for the expense involved. Builders had budgets to advertise in railroad trade journals and were given to producing lithographs and large-size photographs of their products, suitable for office display. But given the date of this catalog and the fact that Rogers had an exhibit in Philadelphia at the United States Centennial Exposition, I wonder if the book was not intended for a larger audience. It may have been produced, in part at least, for distribution at America's first large-scale international trade fair, where national pride was enough to encourage the Rogers firm to dip into its cash reserves in order to subsidize this handsome volume's publication.

If the exact reasons for publishing the 1876 Rogers locomotive catalog are unclear, so too is the identity of the author. It is copyrighted in the name of William S. Hudson, engineering chief of the Rogers works since 1852. The introduction emphasizes technical innovations, which also suggests that Hudson was responsible for the text. The material presented is a pastiche of old trade-paper clippings, blended with engravings and data lifted from standard locomotive texts of the period compiled by Colburn, Clark, and Brown. It appears to be accurately, if not artfully assembled, with the exception of the claim made on page nine about counterbalancing. This idea had been introduced many years before in England; the patent mentioned was never granted, although an application may have been made.

The first catalog issued by an American locomotive builder is believed to be a small pamphlet issued in November 1833 by the American Steam Carriage Company of Philadelphia, better known by its later name of William Norris and Company. The earliest Rogers catalog, at least the oldest known to me, was issued in about 1870. It is a large, undated volume with mounted photographs and a sparse text. Only two copies appear to have survived. The present 1876 issue was followed by a more elaborate volume of the same title in 1886. It features an expanded introductory text by M. N. Forney, editor of the *Railroad Gazette*, and beautifully executed line engravings in place of the collotypes used in the 1876 issue. These cuts have been commonly reproduced on lamp shades, match-book covers, and coffee mugs in recent years but are in no way identified and must have little meaning to their modern-day purchasers, who might never wonder about their origin. The 1886 catalog was reprinted in 1963 and is relatively common in its facsimile edition.

In 1897 a somewhat smaller hardback catalog was published, which deleted the historical introduction and concentrated on current production. It appears to be scarce. Undoubtedly the last publication produced under the Rogers imprint was a small softback booklet of only eighteen pages, published in 1904 for the Saint Louis World's Fair. In less than a year after its appearance, the Rogers firm became part of America's industrial past.

Captions have been keyed to the photographic plates in the Rogers catalog to identify precisely the locomotives reproduced. One might assume that the manufacturer would select his most recent products for inclusion, but one of the engines shown dates from 1860 while many others are a decade out of date. Just why so many Latin American engines are shown is something of a question—it is not representative of Rogers production, which sold predominantly to the domestic market. Perhaps the odd and fanciful products made for railroad lines in Chile, Cuba, and Peru were thought to be of more appeal than the standard designs furnished to North American customers. Construction (or serial) numbers have been included to identify each engine more precisely, but regrettably a major void exists between 1865 and 1872. Numbers marked with a question mark are those assigned by the late Walter Lucas in an effort to reconstruct the maker's original list. The interest of enthusiasts like Lucas and more recent generations of railroad buffs in the products and daily activities of the long-closed Rogers locomotive works would surely please men like Thomas Rogers and William S. Hudson, who devoted their careers to perfecting the locomotive engine.

J. H. W.

CAPTIONS FOR PHOTOGRAPHIC PLATES

Page 36   New Jersey Railroad and Transportation Company. Construction Number [hereafter, C/N] 1262? Completed May 1865.

41   Erie Railway. C/N 1235. February 1865. Broad gauge (6 foot).

45   Erie Railway. C/N 1352? March 1866. Named for the line's master mechanic.

49   Mobile and Montgomery Railroad. C/N 2437. August 1876. Shown in special paint scheme for the Rogers exhibit at the United States Centennial Exposition.

53   Central Railroad of New Jersey. C/N 2416. July 1875.

56   Morris and Essex Railroad. C/N 1516? June 1868.

62   Southern Railway of Chile. C/N 2379. May 1874.

68   Saint Louis, Alton, and Chicago Railroad. C/N 1010. February 1862.

74   Midland Pacific Railway. C/N 2367. December 1873.

79   Nashville and Northwestern Railroad. C/N 946. August 1860.

93   Louisville, Cincinnati, and Lexington Railroad. C/N 1892? July 1871.

97   Puerto Principe Railway (Cuba). C/N 2406. April 1874.

101   Louisville, Cincinnati, and Lexington Railroad. C/N 1530. July 1874.

106   Skaneateles Railroad. C/N 1682? January 1870.

110   Copiapo Railroad (Chile). C/N 1384? July 1866.

113   Tongoy Railway (Chile). C/N 1705? March 1870.

119   Chimbote Huaraz Railway (Peru). C/N 2398. March 1875.

124   Hobson, Hortado, and Company (South America). C/N 2417. July 1875.

129   Cumberland Valley Railroad. C/N 2372. January 1874.

134   Mejia and Arequipa Railway (Peru). C/N 1929? November 1871.

139   Mejia and Arequipa Railway (Peru). C/N 1620? July 1869.

142   Chicago, Burlington, and Quincy Railroad. C/N 1113. November 1863.

147   Copiapo Railway (Chile). C/N 1879? June 1879. One of three light passenger engines.

LOCOMOTIVES

AND

LOCOMOTIVE BUILDING,

BEING

A BRIEF SKETCH OF VARIOUS IMPROVEMENTS IN LOCOMOTIVE BUILDING
DURING THE LAST CENTURY, TOGETHER
WITH A HISTORY OF THE

ORIGIN AND GROWTH

OF THE

ROGERS LOCOMOTIVE AND MACHINE WORKS,

PATERSON, NEW JERSEY,

FROM 1831 TO 1876.

J. S. ROGERS, PRES'T. ⎫
R. S. HUGHES, SEC'Y. ⎬ *PATERSON,*
W. S. HUDSON, SUP'T. ⎭ *N. J.*

R. S. HUGHES, TREAS'R.
44 Exchange Place,
NEW YORK.

NEW YORK:
J. W. PRATT, PRINTER, 73 TO 79 FULTON STREET.
1876.

Thomas Rogers

LOCOMOTIVES

AND

LOCOMOTIVE BUILDING IN AMERICA.

THOMAS ROGERS, the founder of the works at Paterson, N. J., which bear his name, was born March 16th, 1792, in the town of Groton, County of New London, Connecticut. He died in New York City, April 19th, 1856.

He served in the war of 1812, and was a lineal descendant of Thomas Rogers, one of the Pilgrim Fathers who came over to this country from England in the Mayflower.

At the age of sixteen, he was apprenticed to learn the trade of a house carpenter, and in the summer of 1812, he removed to Paterson, N. J., then a small village—but prosperous on account of the demand for American manufactures brought about by the war with Great Britain.

The peace of 1815 reduced many of the manufacturers to bankruptcy. Mr. Rogers was then employed as a journeyman carpenter, and was noticed for his constant application to business, good judgment and force of character.

A few years afterward, Captain Ward, who had been traveling in Europe, where he had witnessed the power-loom in operation, came to Paterson for the purpose of introducing the manufacture of cotton duck. Mr. Rogers was employed in making the patterns for his looms, and taking hold of the idea, he purchased from Captain Ward the patent right for making them.

In 1819, he associated himself with John Clark, Jr., the firm taking the name of Clark & Rogers. They commenced work in the basement story of the Beaver Mill, a building which at an early day had been put up by Mr. Clark's father. Shortly afterward, Mr Rogers visited Mexico where he received large orders for looms, etc.

In 1820, the firm moved into the Little Beaver Mill, and in the following year took into partnership Abram Godwin, Jr., the firm changing the name to Godwin, Rogers & Co. They now commenced spinning cotton and building machinery for that and other purposes.

In 1822, finding their accommodations too limited, they leased Collett's Mill and moved thither. Their business kept increasing, the number of persons employed being sometimes as high as 200. The establishment continued prosperous 'till the summer of 1831, when Mr. Rogers withdrew, taking with him $38,000 as his share of the profits of the concern. This was in the latter part of June.

Having taken a mill-site on the upper raceway, he immediately commenced the erection of the Jefferson Works, which were finished and put in operation before the close of the next year. His design was to occupy the lower stories in building machinery, and the upper stories in spinning cotton. The latter, however, was never commenced, the demand for machinery increasing in a short time to the full capacity of the works.

The Jefferson Works were literally an encroachment on the forest. Between Spruce and Mill streets, all was swamp covered with pines, and, according to all accounts, about as densely inhabited with *snakes* as it is now with human beings.

On the upper race, no factories had been put up, except two little cotton mills and a small machine shop, the latter owned by Messrs. Paul & Beggs.

In the early part of 1832, Mr. Rogers associated with himself Messrs. Morris Ketchum and Jasper Grosvenor, of New York, under the title of Rogers, Ketchum & Grosvenor. About this time, public attention began to be directed to the construction of Railroads and Railroad machinery.

The railroad from Jersey City to Paterson was then approaching completion, the iron work for the Passaic and Hackensack bridges being made by Mr. Rogers. An order was also executed for one hundred sets of wheels and axles for the South Carolina Rail Road.

Mr. Rogers next commenced making wrought iron Tire for car wheels, and, after some difficulties, succeeded.

Preparations for locomotive building had been made by Paul & Beggs, and they had a small engine nearly completed, when the building took fire and was consumed, the locomotive being destroyed.

THE FIRST LOCOMOTIVE AND ITS HISTORY.

In 1835, some buildings were begun by Rogers, Ketchum & Grosvenor, with a view to the manufacture of Locomotives. It was not, however, until eighteen months afterward that the first Locomotive—the "Sandusky," (Fig. 1,) was completed. On the 6th of October, 1837, a trial trip was made from Paterson to Jersey City and New Brunswick and back, Mr. Timothy Smith acting as engineer. The performance of the engine was entirely satisfactory; the gauge of the road was 4 ft. 10 inches, the same as that of the New Jersey Railroad and

ROGERS LOCOMOTIVE AND MACHINE WORKS (1832).

Transportation Co., for which road the engine was intended. It was, however, bought for the Mad River and Lake Erie Railroad by its President, Mr. J. H. James, of Urbana, Ohio, and on the 14th, it was shipped via. Canal and Lake, in charge of Mr. Thomas Hogg, on the schooner "Sandusky." Mr. Hogg had worked upon it from its commencement. It arrived at Sandusky November 17th, 1837, at which time not a foot of track had been laid. The road was built to suit the gauge of the engine, and the Legislature of Ohio passed an act requiring all roads built in that state to be of 4 ft. 10 inches gauge, same as the engine Sandusky.

The engine was used in the construction of the road until the 11th of April, 1838, when regular trips for the conveyance of passengers commenced between Belleview and Sandusky, a distance of 16 miles.

The engineer was Thomas Hogg, who ran the engine for three years, keeping it in repair. The engine continued in service many years, until engines of larger size were required to do the work.

Mr. Hogg subsequently became Master Mechanic of the Mad River Railroad, and continued in that capacity on that and other roads for about thirty years.

The "Sandusky" had cylinders 11 inches diameter by 16 inches stroke, one pair of driving wheels of 4 ft. 6 in. diameter, situated forward of the furnace; the truck had four 30-inch wheels, the eccentrics were outside of the frame, the eccentric rods extending back to the rock shafts, which were situated under the footboard; the smoke pipe was of the bonnet kind, having a deflecting cone curled over at the edges in its centre, so as to deflect the sparks downward, and thus prevent their passing through the wire bonnet, as well as preventing the bonnets wearing out too fast.

COUNTERBALANCING.

In this engine, Mr. Rogers introduced several important improvements, among which we may mention "Counterbalancing," for which he filed a specification in the Patent Office, dated July 12th, 1837. It is thus described in the specification :

"The nature of my improvement consists in providing the section of the wheel opposite to the crank, with sufficient weight to counterbalance the crank and connecting rods, making the resistance of the engine less in starting and in running; also, preventing the irregularity of motion caused by that side of the wheels when the cranks are placed in the usual mode of fitting them up. The irregular motion which arises from not having the cranks and connecting rods balanced, is attended with much injury to the engine, and to the road, and with much loss of power."

The importance of "Counterbalancing" was not recognized as being necessary until several years after it had been introduced by Mr. Rogers, and, when attention was drawn to it, many doubted the necessity of balancing anything more than the cranks.

IMPROVED DRIVING WHEELS.

There was also another remarkable novelty introduced by Mr. Rogers in the "Sandusky." It consisted in making the driving wheels with hollow spokes and hollow rim; the rim on the side opposite to the crank being cast solid. The spokes were oval, and the rim very much of the same shape as at the present time. This kind of driving wheel is in almost universal use in this country at present.

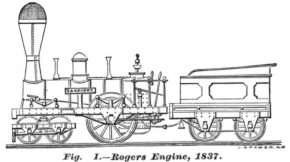

Fig. I.—Rogers Engine, 1837.

It will be seen, from an examination of this engraving, that the engine differs from the English style in having a four-wheeled truck in front, as also in other important particulars already mentioned.

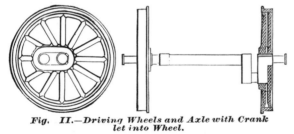

Fig. II.—Driving Wheels and Axle with Crank let into Wheel.

The second locomotive built by Mr. Rogers, was called the "Arresseoh No. 2." It was completed in February, 1838, for the New Jersey Railroad and Transportation Co. It was similar in design to the "Sandusky."

THE "CLINTON," "EXPERIMENT," AND "BATAVIA."

The third engine differed from the first one in its cylinders, which were 10x18 inch stroke, and the gauge was 4 ft. 8½ inches. Both the driving and truck wheels of this engine had hollow oval spokes, and hollow rims with wrought iron tires. This engine, which was named the "Clinton," was built for the Lockport and Niagara Falls Railroad, and was delivered to them in April, 1838. It was run by Wm. E. Cooper until November, 1843, when it was sold to the Toledo and Adrian Railroad for $6500 (the first cost). Mr. Cooper says that when the engine was sold it was considered to be one of the best working engines in existence.

An engine called the "Experiment" was the next or the fourth locomotive turned out. It was made for the South Carolina Railroad, and was delivered in June 1838. This engine differed from the ones previously built at these works, in having a smaller cylinder and longer stroke than usual.

The fifth engine was called the "Batavia." It was made for the Tonawanda Railroad, and was completed in October, 1838.

Fig. III.—Rogers Engine, 1838.

This engine differed from the previous ones in having the driving wheels back of the furnace, which was semi-circular at the rear part, and had a hemispherical top surmounted with a dome. The engine had an arrangement by which a part of the weight of the tender could be transferred to it, so as to increase the adhesion, should it be found necessary to do so.

AMERICAN LOCOMOTIVES IN 1839.

We copy from the American Railroad Journal and Mechanics' Magazine of 1830, an article on American Locomotives. The editor says:

"A few days ago, in company with one of the proprietors, we had the pleasure of a visit to, and inspection of, the very extensive works of Messrs. Rogers, Ketchum & Grosvenor, at Paterson, New Jersey, for the construction of various kinds of machinery. Our attention was, of course, principally directed to the shops for the construction of locomotives, the main building of which is 200 feet long and three stories high, and another of equal length, containing near 50 forges, most of which were in operation, notwithstanding the pressure of the times.

We saw a number of engines in different states of forwardness, and though the general forms are those of 6-wheeled American Engines in general, we were not a little gratified with several minor arrangements, new to us at least, which have been introduced by Mr. Rogers, and to which we shall briefly refer:—

The wire gauze of the smoke pipe is protected by an inverted cone, placed in the axis of the pipe, a few inches below the wire gauze. The base of the cone is curled over so as to scatter the spark over a large portion of the surface of the wire cloth, and to prevent the top of the spark catcher from being burnt out before the rest of the wire cloth is materially injured; it also tends to throw the larger sparks down between the pipe and the casing, and will do something towards diminishing this standing reproach.

The truck frames, whether of wood or iron, were admirably stiffened by diagonal braces, and where the crank axle is used, the large frame is very strongly plated in the manner of Stephenson's engines, the neglect of which till very lately, has been, we are informed, a constant objection to the Philadelphia engines on the Long Island and Troy railroads.

The wheels are of cast iron, with wrought iron tires; the spokes are round, and they, as well as the rims, are hollow, except where the crank axle is used, when the rims are cast solid on one side so as to counterbalance the cranks.

Our readers will probably remember an article on this subject in the Journal, Nos. 7 and 8, page 244 of the present volume, on "side motion or rocking," by G. Heaton, where its success on the Birmingham railroad has been complete.

Mr. Rogers balanced his *first* engine *wheels* two-and-a-half years since, and entered a specification, not with the intention of taking out a patent, but to prevent any one else from doing so; and thus deprive the community of the benefit which Mr. Rogers was desirous of conferring, and which we understand other makers are now availing themselves of. The advantages are fully explained in the article referred to.

When the crank axle is used, the eccentric rods and the cranks of the rockshafts are placed on the *outside*, where they are easily got at, and where they are not crowded into the smallest possible space, as with the ordinary arrangement. For this, also, a specification was entered with the same object as in the preceding case.

But we were most pleased with the arrangement of levers to which the eccentric rods are *fastened*, and thus the *reversing* depends on no contingency, for the rods are *forced* in and out of gear ; a single handle only is required to manage the engine much more rapidly and efficiently than by the ordinary mode. The boilers are 8 ft. long for an 8 ton engine, with 120 flues, the usual length of the former being, we believe, 7 ft., and the number of the latter about 80 or 90 ; by this deviation the area of heating surface is increased, and the heat remains longer in contact with the flues, while the addition to the weight is very trifling compared with the advantages derived from the saving of fuel.

Mr. Baldwin, of Philadelphia, took out a patent some time since for a very ingenious mode of saving half the crank, by inserting the wrist into one of the spokes of the driving wheels, and this has been very closely imitated, by making one complete crank, and by letting one-half of it into a spoke which is cast larger than the others, with a receptacle for the purpose. This latter plan has been adopted by Mr. Rogers and others in this neighborhood, whilst the Boston machinists aim at bringing the two cranks as near together as possible. The relative merits of straight and cranked axles are so well pointed out in Mr. Wood's papers on locomotives in these numbers, that we shall merely beg leave to state that the plan of Mr. Baldwin, and its imitation, appear to us to combine the liability to fracture of the crank axle with the loss of heat, the exposure to accident, and the racking of frame and road ascribed to the straight axle, for the only difference is the thickness of the spoke, the loss of heat is the same in both, the protection against any serious accident is too trifling to be considered, whilst, with the cranks as close together as possible, the cylinders are completely protected.

We offer these remarks as our views merely, and with all due deference to the superior skill of Messrs. Baldwin and Rogers. Mr. Rogers, in common with all other experienced machinists with whom we have conversed, is decidedly opposed to any increase of width of track, beyond 5 ft., with the present weight of engine.

As regards the power of the engines, they are able to slip the wheels when the rails are in the best state ; this they do in common with all good American or English engines, consequently any accounts of extraordinary performance would be worse than superfluous, when we *know* that they will do all that any other engine whatever, with the *same* weight on the driving wheels, possibly *can do*.

As a last remark, we would observe, that there is rather more finish on the engines of Messrs. Rogers, Ketchum & Grosvenor than we are in the habit of seeing ; some parts usually painted black being highly polished. On the whole, we consider their new establishment eminently calculated to add to the reputation of American Locomotives, as it has for many years largely contributed to the character of American machinery for the manufacture of cotton and other objects.

AN EXTRAORDINARY FEAT.

In the same number of the same journal, is the following letter which still further elucidates the subject:

GENTLEMEN :—As you seem to take a deep interest in the success of American locomotives, I will give you a statement for your gratification, in relation to a performance on the New Jersey Railroad a few days since.

ROGERS LOCOMOTIVE AND MACHINE WORKS (1876).

14

Owing to some circumstances, of which I am not informed, it became necessary for a locomotive on the way from Jersey City to New Brunswick, to take, in addition to its own load, the cars attached to another engine, which made the number equal to 24 loaded four-wheeled cars, and with as much apparent ease as could be desired, notwithstanding the grade for four miles is equal to 26 ft. per mile, stopping on the grade to take in passengers, and starting again with the greatest ease. The average speed on the grade was 24½ miles per hour. This may not be in your estimation anything extraordinary, yet, I consider it a performance worth recording, by way of contrast with the *greatest and most extraordinary* performance of a locomotive ever heard of *in those days*, which occurred on the Liverpool and Manchester Railroad in 1829, only ten years ago. *Twenty tons* on a level road at the rate of ten miles per hour, was then considered wonderful! *Astonishing!* even in a country famed for its extraordinary discoveries; yet here, only ten years after, we see an engine built in *this* country too, taking a load probably equal, cars and tender included, to 120 or 180 tons at the rate of 24½ miles per hour, up a grade of 26 ft. per mile. This engine was built, I understand, at Paterson, New Jersey, by Messrs. Rogers, Ketchum & Grosvenor, a concern not yet so well known to this railroad community as manufacturers of locomotives as they ought to be, or as they soon will be, if they continue to turn out such machines as the one above alluded to.

If such have been the improvements in the *past*, what may they not be, permit me to ask, in the next *ten* years?

Pardon me for thus troubling you, but my aim is rather to call attention to the rapid march of improvement in this mode of communication, than to direct attention to any individual or company, although those gentlemen, in my opinion, deserve as manufacturers, much more than I have said of them.

Yours, truly.

JERSEY BLUE.

NEWARK, N. J., DECEMBER 14th, 1839.

THE GROWTH OF LOCOMOTIVE INDUSTRY.

In the year 1838, seven engines were turned out, after which, the production was gradually increased each year until 1854, in which year one hundred and three engines were built.

In 1856, on the decease of Mr. Rogers, the concern was reorganized under a Charter, with the title of the Rogers Locomotive and Machine Works, under the charge of Wm. S. Hudson as Mechanical Engineer and Superintendent, he having been for a number of years previously the assistant of Mr. Rogers.

The Works have been gradually enlarged and improved—(see view of the shops as at present on the opposite page; also, a view of the old works on page 7, from which some idea may be formed as to the great increase in the extent and character of the buildings).

The concern is supplied with greatly improved tools and facilities for turning out accurate work; many of them are of new and approved design, and were manufactured expressly to the order of the Company.

The present capacity for building locomotives is equal to one a day.

VARIOUS STYLES OF LOCOMOTIVES AND VALVE-MOTIONS.

We have introduced illustrations of several styles of locomotives and valve-motions, made by Rogers, Ketchum & Grosvenor, believing they will be of interest.

Fig. IV.—Rogers Eight-Wheeled Engine.
1844.

This engine, (Fig. IV.,) had eccentrics on the back axle, the pumps were full stroke, worked from the cross-heads, the springs were over the back axle bearings, and also in the centre of levers extending from driving axle to the centre of the truck on each side of the engine. The truck was pivoted, and turned upon a centre pin fixed to the boiler; the arrangement did not give satisfaction, and was altered after a short trial.

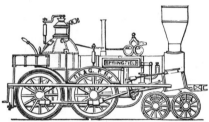

Fig. V.—Rogers Eight-Wheeled Engine.
1845.

This style of engine, (Fig. V.,) had equalizing levers, between the driving-wheel springs; the truck had side bearings and springs over the sides of truck; the pumps had short stroke, worked from cross head as shown.

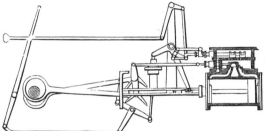

Fig. VI.—V Hooks and Independent Variable Cut-off on separate face. 1845 and 1846.

Figure VI. shows a valve motion for locomotives, designed and used by Thomas Rogers as early as 1845. It serves to show the thought he was giving at that date to the subject of working steam expansively.

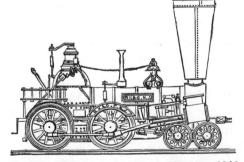

Fig.VII.—Rogers Eight-Wheeled Engine, 1846.
V Hooks and Independent Cut-off on
the back of Main Valve.

Figure VII. shows an engine with the driving wheels spread well apart. It had V hooks and independent cut-off on the back of the main valves; this was a favorite kind of engine for many years.

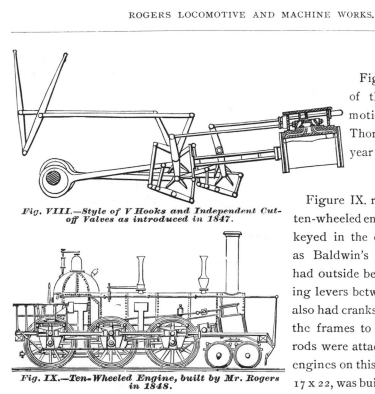

Fig. VIII.—Style of V Hooks and Independent Cut-off Valves as introduced in 1847.

Figure VIII. shows one of the styles of valve motions introduced by Thomas Rogers, in the year 1847.

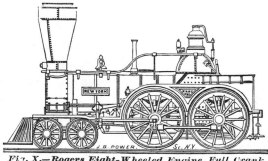

Fig. IX.—Ten-Wheeled Engine, built by Mr. Rogers in 1848.

Figure IX. represents a plan of ten-wheeled engine, with half crank keyed in the driving wheel, same as Baldwin's plan. The engine had outside bearings and equalizing levers between the springs; it also had cranks on the axles outside the frames to which the coupling rods were attached. A number of engines on this plan, with cylinders 17 x 22, was built for the New York and Erie Railway. They all had independent cut-off valves.

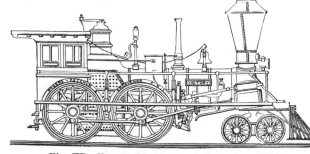

Fig. X.—Rogers Eight-Wheeled Engine, Full Crank, 1848.

Figure X. represents an engine with full crank; the steam chests were inclined sidewise, so that the valves could be readily got at. This was one of the improvements introduced by Thomas Rogers. The engine had V Hooks and Independent Cut-off Valves, and was built for the Paterson and Hudson River Railroad.

Fig. XI.—Rogers Eight-Wheeled Engine, 1850. Shifting Link Motion.

On this style of Engine, (Fig. XI.,) the shifting-link motion was introduced. Thomas Rogers was one of its earliest advocates, and did more towards its successful introduction on American locomotives than any other person. He was not only an early, but an earnest advo-

cate of it, at a time when some people were styled fools for so doing ; neverthe-
less, time has amply proved all that he claimed for it, viz : that it is the most
simple and efficient device ever made for the purpose.

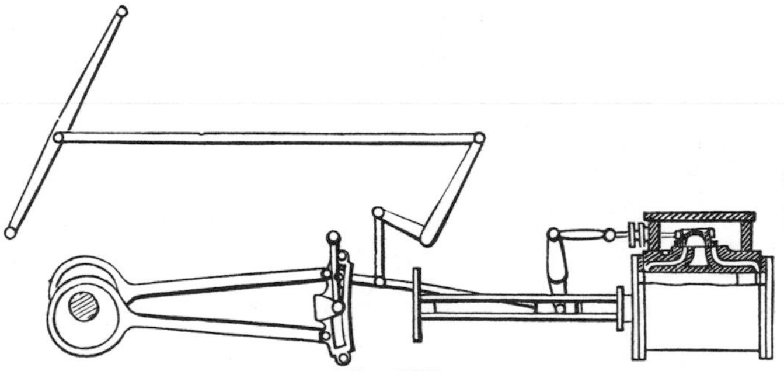

Figure XII. shows a
suspended link, as made
by Thomas Rogers, in
1849.

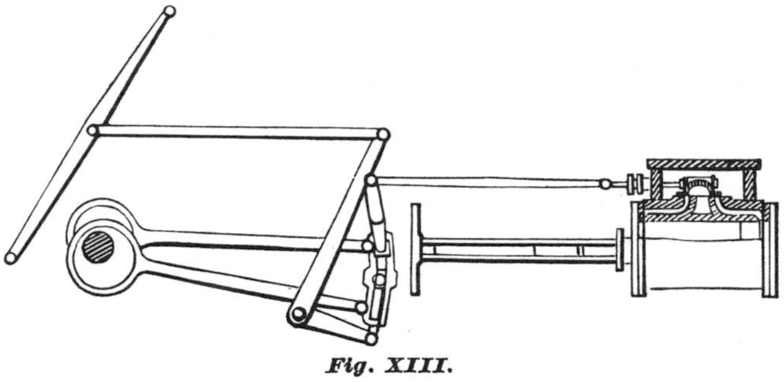

Fig. XII.

Figure XIII. shows a
Shifting-link Motion, as
made by Thomas Rogers
in 1850.

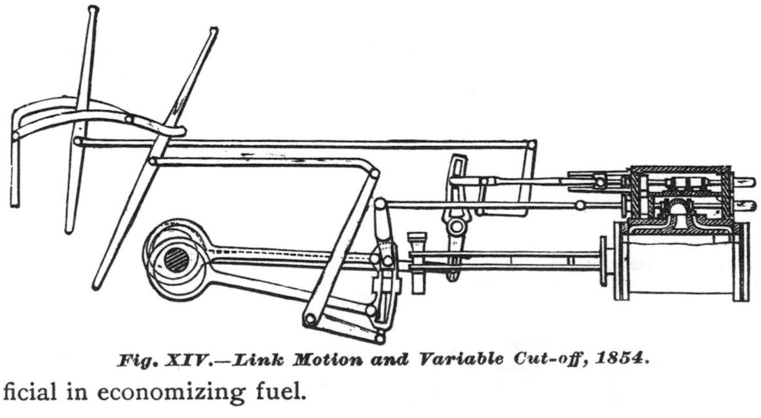

Fig. XIII.

Figure XIV. re-
presents a combi-
nation of link
motion, with an
independent
graduated cut-
off. It was intro-
duced on several
locomotives, and
was found bene-

Fig. XIV.—Link Motion and Variable Cut-off, 1854.

ficial in economizing fuel.

THE "MᶜNEILL."

The first locomotive on the Paterson and Hudson River Railroad was
called the "McNeill." It was ordered by Judge Dickerson, then President of
the road, in the year 1833, to be as good as possible, without regard to cost, and
was built by Geo. Stephenson. It arrived, and was put in operation in the year
1834. The cylinders were 9 inches diameter, by 18 inches stroke, and one pair

of driving wheels 5 feet in diameter, which were behind the fire-box. The axle was cranked, and the cranks were close to the wheels; there was room for the connecting rods to pass by the outside of the furnace. The front end was supported by a four-wheeled truck; the fire-box and tubes were of copper.

This engine continued in use many years, and was said to be very fast; it was finally sold to a Western Road, the business on the Paterson and Hudson River Road having grown beyond the engine's capacity.

INSIDE vs. OUTSIDE CONNECTED ENGINES.

Thomas Rogers, soon after commencing the building of locomotive engines, became convinced that inside connected engines, with crank axles, were inferior in many respects to outside connected ones, besides being more expensive to build and to keep in repair; he, also, became satisfied that in the matter of steadiness, the inside-connected had no advantage over the outside-connected engine, and that, with proper counterbalancing, the latter could be run as fast as required without any injurious oscillation; and also, that it required more skill to properly counterbalance inside connected engines than outside ones. Therefore, he was an earnest advocate of this style of engine, and recommended outside connected engines as better than inside connected ones.

In the early inside connected engines, Mr. Rogers followed the plan which is still used in England, viz   putting the cranks for parallel or coupling rods opposite to the main cranks. He soon found that this arrangement, while it had some advantages, such as requiring less counterbalance, caused the journals of the driving axles to wear oval; he therefore adopted the plan of putting the cranks for both main and outside rods on the same side of the centre of the axle.

THE PREVENTION OF CRACKING BOILER PLATES.

In the construction of locomotive boilers, Mr. Rogers found that, in flanging the sheets, a great strain was put upon them, so much so as to endanger their cracking while being riveted together, or, if they did not crack when being riveted, they were likely to do so after being a short time in use. To remedy this evil, he adopted the plan of taking out the strains—caused by flanging, punching and hammering—by heating the sheets red-hot after they were prepared to be riveted together, and then allowing them to cool slowly. This plan was found so effectual with iron, that it was a very rare thing to have sheets crack when in use; the same method was afterward adopted with steel sheets, and it has no doubt been the means of preventing many of these sheets from cracking, which would otherwise have done so while being worked soon afterward; still, it is a well-known fact, that our knowledge of steel is not yet such that we can insure steel furnaces lasting for any great length of time without being liable to crack.   We have no doubt, however, that the difficulty will be overcome, either by our being able to get a better material that is capable of withstanding all the strains without cracking, or by putting the material in such a shape as will accommodate all the expansions and contractions to which it is subjected while in use ; or, to so proportion the water spaces as to allow better circulation to carry off the heat, thus preventing undue strains, either from expansion or contraction.   If the latter plan is properly carried out, we feel confident that it will very materially add to the life of steel furnaces.   We do not, however, expect that it will prove effective against the failure of poor steel, or steel not suited to the purpose.

The plan of placing the flues of the boilers in vertical rows, is also one conceived by Mr. Rogers, as it gave more freedom, and offered less obstruction to the circulation of the water than the arrangement then in use.

EXPANSION PLATES.

Thomas Rogers was the first builder of locomotives to use expansion plates, so as to relieve both the boiler and frame from the strains due to the lengthening of the boiler when under steam, as well as to provide for its shortening when cold or cooling down.   The system he adopted is now in general use.

THE "MOGUL."

The style of engine called the "Mogul," was first built at these works in the year 1863.   It was made with two-wheeled Bissell trucks ; swing links, on the plan of Mr. Smith's, instead of the Bissell inclined planes were afterward used.   Another important improvement was introduced, (patented by W. S. Hudson, the superintendent of the works).   It consisted in placing an arrangement of equalizing levers between the two-wheeled truck and the front driving wheels, whereby both truck and driving wheels maintain their proper portion of the weight, and accommodate themselves to the vertical, as well as to the lateral, motion required to enable the engine to pass over uneven tracks, and around curves with ease as well as with perfect safety

WHAT ONE ENGINE DID.

The following data with reference to the performance of a six-wheel (all drivers) freight engine (Fig. XV.), built by Rogers, Ketchum & Grosvenor, in the year 1854, will be found of interest.

Editor of American Railway Times :—

BUFFALO, JANUARY 23, 1859.

Fig. XV.—Rogers Six-Wheeled Engine, the same as Engine "Vulcan," 1854.

The engine "Vulcan," of the Buffalo and State Line Railway, came out of the shop after a general overhauling, on the 15th of December, 1856, and made fifteen trips of 90 miles each, 1350 miles, and hauling 435 cars in that month.

In the year 1857, this engine made three hundred and twelve trips, of 90 miles each, hauling 8509 cars; in the year 1858, this engine made two hundred and ninety trips, hauling 9351 cars.

RECAPITULATION.

				CARS HAULED.	AVERAGE TRAIN.
1856,	15 trips,	1,350 miles.		435	29 cars.
1857,	312 "	28,080 "		8,509	27½ "
1858,	290 "	26,100 "		9,351	32¼ "
Aggregate,	617 "	55,530 "		18,295	Average, 30 "

These were all eight-wheeled cars, and, when loaded, (which averaged two-thirds of the time) carried ten tons. The cars weigh on an average eight tons, so that the average weight of train would be

30 cars of eight tons each	240 tons.
Average load, 10 tons, less one-third . . .	200 "
Gross weight of train . .	440 "

The aggregate cost of repairs in the two years and fifteen days was 1140 dollars, and, per mile run, two-and-a-half cents.

This engine is a six-wheeler, all drivers, weighs 27 tons in working order, drivers four feet two inches, chilled cast-iron tires, carried 120 lbs. steam only, has a link and direct action-valve motion, cylinders 16x22.

The road has a good line, but one grade of 36 feet per mile for two miles—part of it on a curve, several grades of 31 feet, and four reverse curves in quick succession (at Harbor Creek) of 1350 feet radius, on a grade of 15 feet to the mile. The largest train drawn was fifty-four cars, the smallest, twelve cars, and the average was as above. If we multiply these 18,295 cars hauled, by 88 miles, the actual length of the road, we shall have one car hauled 1,609,960 miles, and if we call twelve-and-a-half cents the average earnings of a car per mile, we shall have the sum of $201,245 as the actual freight earnings of this engine in a few days over two years, and the earnings per mile run by the engine, will be three dollars and seventy-five cents, which is more than double the earnings per mile run, of any freight engine I have ever seen any record of. I also send you herewith the precise earnings of another engine of the same sort, when there was an effort made to make a good show :

Miles run in sixteen days	1,632
Money earned in sixteen days	$9,715.54
Money earned per mile run	$5.95

The average number of cars in each train was thirty.

Now, Mr. Editor, it is an old adage and a good one—"to give the devil his due." To the Railway public, it is not of the slightest consequence where, or by whom any particular style of engine was gotten up, but it is of great importance to this same public, to get at all the facts, and to have and use common sense in deciding upon the real merits of this or any other style of engine.

I am truly yours,

AN OLD ENGINEMAN.

THE EARLIER RAILWAYS.

Railways of wood were first used about the year 1670, for conveying coals from the mines to the river Tyne, in Northumberland, England · the next improvement was the adoption of iron instead of wood for the rails—this change, which enabled one horse to draw double his previous load, was made about the year 1767. Cast-iron tram rails were first used about the year 1776. In 1789 cast iron edge rails were used by Mr. Jessup.

Oval sloped rails were first used on the road of Lord Penryhn, for conveying slate from the quarries in Caermarthenshire to Port Penryhn in Wales. The wheels were hollowed on the rim ; the gauge was twenty-four inches. This was in the year 1801.

Cast iron rails, with concave surfaces, were patented in the year 1803.

In the year 1802, Messrs. Trevethick & Vivian patented a plan of locomotive which was (ten years afterward) put into operation. In the boiler of this engine, a fusible plug was employed.

In a patent granted to James Watt, in the year 1784, he gave an account of the adaptation of his mechanism to the propulsion of land carriages. He proposed that the boiler should be made of wooden staves, joined together and fastened with iron hoops like a cask, but Mr. Watt never put this idea into practice.

In the year 1811, a patent was taken out by John Blenkinsop, of Middleton, Yorkshire, England, for certain mechanical means by which the conveyance of coal and other articles was facilitated, and the expense attending the conveyance of the same was rendered less than before. It consisted in the application of a rack or toothed rail on one side of the road from end to end. Into this rack a toothed wheel was worked by the steam engine, the revolutions of which produced the necessary motion without being liable to slip in descending steep inclined planes. Several Blenkinsop Engines were made by Fenton, Murray & Wood, of Leeds, England, in 1812 and 1813.

THE CHAPMAN LOCOMOTIVE.

In the year 1812, Messrs. Wm. & E. W. Chapman of Durham, England, set at work (on the Railway leading from Mr. Lambton's collieries to the river

Wear), a remarkable locomotive—(see Fig. XVI). It is thus described in the Encyclopedia, by Luke Hebert, in the year 1836: "The boiler consisted of a large cylinder of the Trevethick kind, with the furnace, and a double return flue passing through it to the chimney, situated on one side of the fire-door, opposite to which was a chest containing fuel. The steam-chamber was a large vertical cylinder, from which proceeded, laterally, a pipe to conduct the steam to the two vertical cylinders fixed on either side of the boiler, the motion of the rods whose lower extremities worked two revolving cranks, carrying on their axis spur gears, which through the medium of a train of toothed wheels shown, gave simultaneous motion to all the running wheels. The weight of this engine, with fuel and water, was six tons; it drew after it eighteen loaded coal wagons weighing fifty-four tons, up a grade of 46 feet per mile, at the rate of four miles an hour. The power of the engine was applied to all the running wheels, and was capable of drawing the eighteen wagons after they were in motion, but considerable slipping took place at starting."

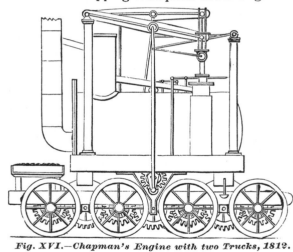

Fig. XVI.—Chapman's Engine with two Trucks, 1812.

We have introduced this notice of the earliest experiment made with the engine of the Messrs. Chapman, because it exemplifies in the clearest manner, that precise inclination of the plane upon which the *smooth* wheels of a locomotive bearing a certain weight will slip around without advancing the machine. It also proves the necessity in such cases, of increasing the friction of the opposing surfaces, either by augmenting the weight or by some contrivance resembling those suggested by Trevethick in his specifications, which Dr. Lardner repeatedly in the course of his work treats as "an absurd attempt to remedy an *imaginary* difficulty."

It will be noticed that this engine had two 4-wheel trucks.

THE RACK RAIL DISPENSED WITH.

Wood, in his treatise upon Railroads, mentions that, in the year 1814, an engine on Blenkinsop's plan, was constructed at the Killingworth Colliery by Geo. Stephenson, and tried upon that railroad, when the engine had been at work a short time, it was found that there was sufficient adhesion between the wheels and rails to do the work without the rack rail

In the year 1820 John Birkinshaw, of Bedlington Iron Works, Durham, England, took out a patent for making wrought iron rails of various forms.

AN ELEVATED RAILWAY.

In 1821 H. R. Palmer proposed making a Railway consisting of a single set of rails, elevated on posts, and carried in a straight line across the country, the carriages to be in pairs, suspended on each side of the rails, like panniers on each side of a mule. A railway on this principle was made at Cheshunt, in Hertfordshire, (in the year 1825,) from the town across the marshes to the river Lea, for shipment. About this time, it was proposed to use wind acting on sails, as the motive power. In the year 1826, Robert Stephenson patented a method of allowing the wheels of carriages on Railways to revolve independently of each other.

RADIUS RODS.

In the year 1827 Walter Hancock turned his attention to the construction of locomotives for ordinary roads, and he introduced into some of his engines, radius rods between the crank shaft and the shaft having the driving wheels upon it, in order to allow the driving wheels to move up and down according to the condition of the road, without altering the length of the connecting rods, so as to cause increased friction; he also used a similar device between the axles where two pairs were connected together.

LOCOMOTIVE vs. FIXED ENGINES.

The Liverpool and Manchester Railway was commenced in the year 1826, under the direction of Geo. Stephenson as engineer. After mature deliberation, the management determined to have *locomotive* in preference to *fixed* engines for motive power, provided the former could be made sufficiently powerful, and that the weight were not so great as to injure the rails; also, ones that would not emit smoke.

COMPETITION INVITED.

In 1829 a reward was offered for the best engine under the following conditions, viz: to consume its own smoke, to draw three times its own weight at ten miles an hour, with not over 50 lbs. pressure of steam on the boiler, to have two safety valves, (one locked), the boiler to be supported on springs, and to rest on six wheels if it weighed more than four-and-a-half tons; height to top of chimney, not over fifteen feet, weight, with water in the boiler, not to exceed six tons, (less preferred), boiler proved to three times the working pressure, and not to cost more than £550.

THE "ROCKET."

The trial resulted in the success of the "Rocket," (Fig. XXII), and the prize of £500 was awarded to George Stephenson. The superiority of the "Rocket" was, in a great measure, due to the boiler having small tubes, and to the blast from the exhaust steam enabling the engine to generate steam as fast as required. It is claimed that the flue boiler was suggested by Henry Booth, the treasurer of the Company.

THE TUBULAR SYSTEM INVENTED.

Mr. Lobert, a French writer, states, that in the year 1829 two engines, built by Stephenson, were put on the St. Etienne Railway in France. On trial their average speed was four miles an hour. M. Seguin, the engineer of the road, resolved to apply a device of his own to some engines he was to construct on the model of Stephenson's; this device he had matured in 1827, and patented in February, 1828. "It consisted in subdividing the current of hot air into streamlets which flowed through a series of tubes immersed in the water of the boiler."

This plan he carried out, but the difficulty of getting the smoke through the tubes required the use of a blowing fan; with this aid the boiler made steam much faster than the ones in the engines built by Stephenson. From the foregoing, it appears that the tubular system of boilers was invented in both England and France at the same time. From this time the march of the locomotive was rapid.

VARIOUS IMPROVEMENTS.

In the year 1833 Robert Stephenson took out a patent for leaving off the flanges of the driving wheels, and using flanges on the leading and trailing wheels only.

In the year 1835 Mr. Henry Booth patented a compound for lubricating the axles of railway carriages and wagons. It consisted of oil, tallow or grease and water, with a mixture of soda, making a sort of semi soap; this compound is still extensively used for the same purpose in England.

On the opening of the Liverpool and Manchester Railway, Mr. Huskisson was unfortunately run over, and a locomotive conveying his wounded body, a distance of fifteen miles, ran at the rapid rate of thirty-six miles per hour.

THE INVENTION OF THE STEAM BLAST.

Richard Trevethick, in his evidence before a committee of the House of Commons, on steam carriages in 1831, claims to have been the inventor of the steam blast. He says—"The first locomotive ever seen was one I set to work in 1804, which performed its work to admiration, a correct copy of which is now in use on the railroad. The fire is enclosed in the boiler, surrounded with water, and a forced draught is created by the steam for the purpose of working on the roads without a high chimney." This claim has been disputed, and the credit given to Geo. Stephenson, and also to Timothy Hackworth.

D. K. Clark says, that the blast pipe applied in the Royal George locomotive in 1827, is said to have been the first application of it as a promoter of combustion.

EXHAUST PIPES AND STEAM BLOWERS.

Variable exhaust pipes were first used by Pambour, in his experiments on the Liverpool and Manchester Railway, in the year 1835. A variable Exhaust for locomotive engines was patented by John Grey, in 1838.

We find in a specification of a patent granted the Earl of Dundonald, in 1835, that he described as part of his invention, a Steam Blower, using live steam from the boiler to blow up the chimney of a locomotive engine, for getting up steam rapidly. This system is still in use at present, with very little, if any improvement.   (Figure XVII).

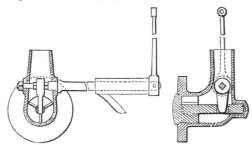

Fig. XVII.—Steam Blower, 1852 or '53.

The engine "Utility," designed by A. F. Smith, Superintendent of the Cumberland Valley Railroad, had a steam blower which we illustrate.

This engine was built by Seth Wilmarth, of the Union Works, South Boston, Mass.

INDIA RUBBER SPRINGS.

In the patent granted the Earl of Dundonald, in 1835, he includes making boilers to use water in the tubes instead of outside, and with a system of circulating plates. He also described as a part of his invention applicable to locomotive carriages for quick traveling on railways, piles or heaps of india rubber, or cork, or other suitable substance in cakes, laid one upon another, jointly, with or in lieu of metallic springs, for sustaining the weight with which such carriages are loaded ; such piles of elastic substances to be enclosed, as it were, within inverted boxes, resting on the contents, and the weight to be borne upon the lids or covers of such boxes,—they will then form an elastic or springy bearing. Such boxes may be applied over the axles of the wheels of the carriages.

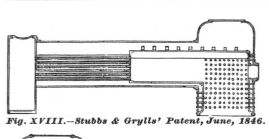

Fig. XVIII.—Stubbs & Grylls' Patent, June, 1846.

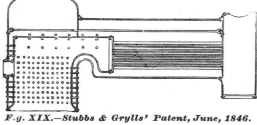

F.g. XIX.—Stubbs & Grylls' Patent, June, 1846.

We find in a Patent granted to Stubbs & Grylls, of Llanelly, South Wales, in the year 1847, an account of improvements in locomotive boilers, showing two plans, with combustion chambers. (Figures XVIII and XIX.

A SAVING OF WEIGHT IN BOILERS.

In a patent granted to John McConochie and Louis Claude, in the year 1848, is a method of saving weight in the boilers of locomotives without diminishing the heating surface. It consists in tapering a part of the furnace and outside shell, both rearward and downward, and instead of using crown bars, the sheets are stayed together with screwed staybolts, the same as on the sides.

CAST IRON THIMBLES A REMEDY FOR LEAKY FLUES.

Twenty-five or thirty years ago a great deal of trouble was experienced on locomotive engines with leaky flues; it was a constant source of annoyance, and every few days, some one had to go into the furnace to hammer or caulk up the ends of the flues and thimbles, (the flues at that time were either copper or brass, and the thimbles were of wrought iron).

In the year 1850, W. S. Hudson, then Master Mechanic of the Attica and Buffalo Railroad, conceived the idea, that if cast iron thimbles were substituted for wrought iron, it would remedy this standing reproach. Acting on this idea, he proceeded to verify it,—first by taking a thimble of each kind, wrought and cast iron, turning them accurately to a gauge, then heating them red hot, measuring them, and noting the expansion of each; afterward, cooling them in water, and again measuring them. This process of heating, cooling and measuring was repeated twelve times or more, when the wrought thimble was found to be appreciably less than at first, and the cast iron thimble appreciably larger. It was noticed that the former thimbles expanded more than the latter when red hot; this was as anticipated.

To carry this idea into practice, a locomotive with leaky flues was taken :—
All the thimbles were taken out, the flues carefully expanded, and new thimbles
put in.   One-half, or all on one side of the centre line of the flue sheet vertically,
were of wrought iron, and the other half were all of cast iron.   At the end of
the first trip, when the boiler was cooling down, it was found that all the flues
with wrought iron thimbles were leaking, whereas, at the same time, all those
opposite to them, with cast iron thimbles, were tight.   The wrought thimbles
were then taken out and cast iron ones put in their places, when all stopped
leaking and so continued, the engine doing duty daily, without any more trouble
from leaky flues.   The attention of Thomas Rogers was called to the fact, and
he began to use cast iron thimbles with a like result.   Mr. Rogers called the
attention of John Brandt, then in charge of the motive power on the Erie Railway, to the subject ; he, also, immediately tried cast iron thimbles, and found
the result as stated above, and hence, their use spread and became almost
universal ; few, except those who had experience in the matter at that time, can
now realize how much annoyance and expense were saved by the change.

THE PARSON'S RENCONTRE WITH A RUNAWAY ENGINE.

An amusing story is told in relation to a small locomotive, (Fig. XX),
made by William Murdock, in the year 1784.   It appeared many years ago in
the *Railroad Advocate*, edited by Holly & Colburn.

"At Redruth, in England, a worthy pastor was returning from visits to his flock, when he saw
before him a strange nondescript, as large as a black ram, with eyes flashing fire, and breathing very
hard, running furiously toward his shins; providentially, he sprang aside, and before his assailant could
stop and turn 'round upon him, he had run to such a distance as gave hope of deliverance, when he
came full butt against a man running in the opposite direction. 'Run for your life !—back! back!'
cried the parson. 'Have you seen my steamer?' asked the stranger. 'I've seen the evil spirit himself!
run, run !' · 'By Jove !' exclaimed the stranger, 'How far ahead is she?' The tone of this question,
and the company of a human creature, in some measure dispelled the fright of the faithful man, and

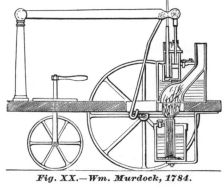

admonished him that he, if any one, should have
courage to face the powers of darkness; so he turned,
and ran after the stranger, who, as he thought, by
mistake had taken the wrong direction. They soon
came up to the object of their pursuit, which had
got into a ditch, and was roaring terrifically. The
stranger, to the astonishment of the parson, seized
and dragged the fiery monster to the road.

'She got away from me, Sir. I was giving her a
try, this bit of road being good for a run.' 'Oh
goodness ! well, she is yours then? Pray, what is
she? 'A steamer, Sir, I call her; she is a little

Fig. XX.—Wm. Murdock, 1784.

experiment of mine—gotten up to try whether Mr. Watt's idea of running coaches by steam can be carried out. I think it can, Sir, if money can be got for it.' 'Indeed! Indeed! Pray, my dear sir, who may you be?' 'I am William Murdock, sir, at your service, a mechanical engineer, superintending the erection of pumping engines for Boulton & Watt, in the mines hereabouts.'"

THE FIRST RAILWAY CAR.

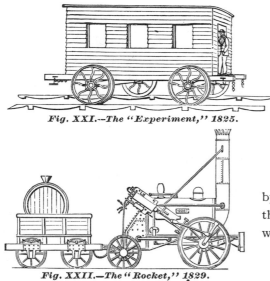

Fig. XXI.--The "Experiment," 1825.

We also show (Figure XXI,) the first Railway car ever used for carrying passengers. It was on the Stockton & Darlington Railroad, in 1825.

The "Rocket," (Figure XXII), built by R. Stephenson & Co., was put on the Liverpool and Manchester Railway, in the year 1829.

Fig. XXII.—The "Rocket," 1829.

SOME FAMOUS LOCOMOTIVES.

The illustrations of the "Stourbridge Lion," the "Best Friend," and the "Tom Thumb," were copied from "The History of the First Locomotives in America," by Wm. H. Brown, 1871.

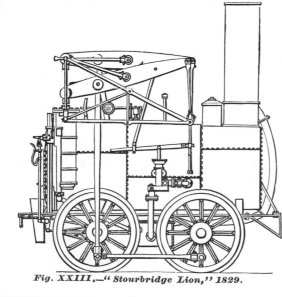

The "Stourbridge Lion," (Figure XXIII,) is said to have been the first Locomotive imported into America, and was ordered by Mr. Horatio Allen, for the Delaware and Hudson Canal and Railroad Company. It was tried at Honesdale, Pennsylvania, in August, 1829, and was found to be too heavy, having nearly two tons weight on each wheel.

Fig. XXIII.—" Stourbridge Lion," 1829.

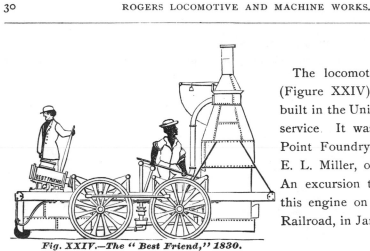

Fig. XXIV.—The " Best Friend," 1830.

The locomotive "Best Friend," (Figure XXIV), was the first one built in the United States for actual service. It was made at the West Point Foundry, in New York, for E. L. Miller, of Charleston, S. C. An excursion trip was made with this engine on the South Carolina Railroad, in January, 1831.

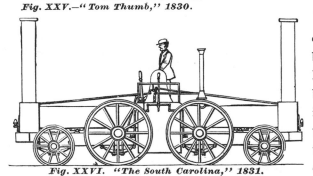

Fig. XXV.—"Tom Thumb," 1830.

A small experimental locomotive called "Tom Thumb," (Figure XXV), was built by Peter Cooper. It was tried on the Baltimore and Ohio Road, in August, 1830. It was too small for much of a ioad, but served to show what might be done with a larger and more perfectly constructed machine.

Fig. XXVI. "The South Carolina," 1831.

A locomotive, (Fig. XXVI), designed by Horatio Allen, was built for the South Carolina Railroad in the year 1831. The boiler had two barrels extending each way from the furnace which was in the middle of the boiler. The engine had eight wheels arranged in two trucks. It was built at the West Point Foundry Shops, New York City.

Fig. XXVII. "The "De Witt Clinton," 1831.

The "De Witt Clinton," (Figure XXVII), was the third locomotive built by the West Point Foundry Co. It was made for the Mohawk and Hudson Railroad, and was ordered by John B. Jervis, Esq. The first excursion trip with passengers, drawn by the "De Witt Clinton," was made from Albany to Schenectady, August 9th, 1831.

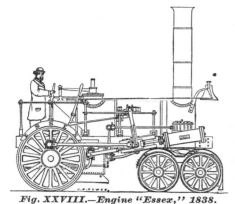

Fig. XXVIII.—Engine "Essex," 1838.

The locomotive engine, "Essex," (Figure XXVIII), was built by Seth Boyden, of Newark, N. J. The engine was a novelty, as will be apparent by an inspection of the drawing. The valves were worked without eccentrics, motion being given to them by levers connected to the crossheads, each one communicating motion to the valve of the opposite cylinder. Seth Boyden was a man of genius, and made many important inventions. He was a pioneer in producing cheap brads for joiners ; and of patent leather, malleable iron, daguerreotypes, &c. He also assisted Prof. Morse in his early experiments with the electric telegraph. We have mentioned only a few of the many branches of industry which Mr. Boyden's inventions tended to bring to perfection.

GRAY'S EXPANSION GEAR.

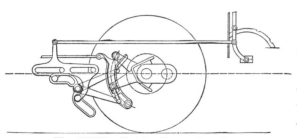

Fig. XXIX.—Gray's Expansion Gear.

From D. K. Clark's Railway Machinery, page 25, we take the following :

"In all the individuals of the class of variable expansion gear with a single valve, the travel is varied by means of mechanism external to the valve chest.

Gray's gearing, (Figure XXIX), as applied on the Liverpool and Manchester Railway, is the first that was in that country (England) applied to locomotives. The pin of the eccentric rod works in a segmental lever, curved to the radius of the rod, the upper end of which is linked to the valve spindle. Thus, the lever being concentric with the fore-rod at the beginning of the stroke, the rod may be raised or lowered in the slot of the lever, to any required distance from the fulcrum, which, of course, regulates the travel of the valve, while the lead remains unchanged. The reversing mechanism consists principally of a wrought iron frame, which slides horizontally on two fixed pivots, and carries rollers, which, working in grooved levers linked to the eccentric-rods, place these rods in and out of gear with the segmental lever, as required. The action of reversing, is, in this mechanism, very suddenly performed in the quick bends of the grooved levers, and accordingly, in practice, very great manual power was demanded for the operation. To Mr. Gray is due the merit of the first application of the principle of varying expansion, by variation of travel, whether in locomotive, land, or marine engines—a principal of primary importance at the present day, though originally embodied in a complicated and inconvenient piece of gear.

In the perusal of the foregoing pages, the reader having any degree of fondness whatever for mechanical studies or pursuits, cannot have failed to note that the growth and development of invention, as herein recorded, have been steadily progressive ; each decade apparently achieving improvements before undreamed of, and adding its *quota* to the discoveries of its predecessor. Nor is there any reason, in view of this fact, for doubting that great as is the progress already made, still greater, and more wonderful rewards await the inventor of the future. In the hope that this work may contribute its share of impetus toward bringing about such a result, its author respectfully commits it to the care and consideration of its readers.

PREFATORY.

————•━•————

The loads that can be drawn by each class of Locomotives given in the tables are in addition to the weight of the Engine and Tender, and are in tons of 2000 pounds.

In calculating the power of Locomotives in the annexed tables, the pressure of the steam is taken at 130 lbs. per square inch, and the cutting off at 50 and 70 per cent. of stroke.

Engines under favorable circumstances will draw greater loads than those given in the tables.

EXPLANATION OF TERMS.

		Driving Wheels	Truck Wheels
P.	Passenger Loco. Eng. with	4	4
F.	Freight " " "	4	4
M.	Mogul " " "	6	2
S.	Switching " " "	4 or 6	
S. T.	Switching Tank " "	4 or 6	
T. W.	Ten Wheel " "	6	4
D. E.	Double Ender " "	4, 6 or 8	4 or 6
M. T.	Mogul Tank " "	6	2
M.Ten	Mogul Tender " "	6	10
I. E.	Inspector's Engine	2	2 Leading
F. T.	Freight Tank	4	4 Truck
P. T.	Passenger Tank	2	4

The tables contain the size of cylinders and wheels, the pressure of steam, the point of cut off, and the loads that can be hauled in each case

CLASS P.

LOCOMOTIVE ENGINES FOR PASSENGER SERVICE.

GENERAL DESIGN ILLUSTRATED ON PAGE 36.

CYLINDERS.

Diameter of cylinders	10 inches.
Length of stroke	18 "

DRIVING-WHEELS.

Diameter of drivers	37 to 49 inches.

TRUCK.

FOUR-WHEELED CENTRE-BEARING TRUCK.

Diameter of wheels	20 to 24 inches.

WHEEL-BASE.

Total wheel-base	17 ft.
Rigid " (distance between driving-wheel centres) .	6 ft. 6 inches.

TENDER.

ON SIX OR EIGHT WHEELS.

Capacity of tank	1000 to 1200 gallons.

WEIGHT OF ENGINE IN WORKING ORDER.

On drivers	21,000 lbs.
On truck	13,000 "
Total weight of engine about . . .	34,000 "

LOAD.

IN ADDITION TO ENGINE AND TENDER.

130 lbs. initial pressure, cylinders 10x18—49 inch wheel		Cyls. 10x18. 37 in. wheel.	
Admission	50%. 70%	50%.	70%.
On a level	403 . 527	551 .	715
" 20 ft. grade	178 . 237	249 .	327
" 40 "	106 . 145	153 .	204
" 60 "	71 . 100	107 .	145
" 80 "	51 . 74	78 .	109
" 100 "	37 . 56	60 .	86

CLASS P.

LOCOMOTIVE ENGINES FOR PASSENGER SERVICE.

GENERAL DESIGN ILLUSTRATED ON PAGE 36.

CYLINDERS.

Diameter of cylinders . . . . . . 11 inches.
Length of stroke . . . . . 18 or 20 inches.

DRIVING-WHEELS

Diameter of drivers . . . . 37 to 49 inches.

TRUCK.
FOUR-WHEELED CENTRE-BEARING TRUCK.

Diameter of wheels . . . . . 20 to 24 inches.

WHEEL-BASE.

Total wheel-base . . . . 17 ft. to 18 ft.
Rigid " (distance between driving-wheel centres) . 6 ft. 6 inches.

TENDER.
ON SIX OR EIGHT WHEELS.

Capacity of tank . . . . 1400 gallons.

WEIGHT OF ENGINE IN WORKING ORDER.

On drivers . . . . 23,000 lbs.
On truck . . . . 15,000 "

Total weight of engine about . . . 38,000 "

LOAD.
IN ADDITION TO ENGINE AND TENDER.

130 lbs. initial pressure, cylinders 11x18—49 inch wheel		Cyls. 11x20. 37 in. wheel.	
Admission	50%.	70%	50%.	70%.
On a level .	499	648	747	968
" 20 ft. grade	225	296	340	460
" 40 "	136	184	210	279
" 60 "	94	129	147	197
" 80 "	69	97	109	150
" 100 "	52	75	84	118

CLASS P.

LOCOMOTIVE ENGINES FOR PASSENGER SERVICE.

GENERAL DESIGN ILLUSTRATED ON PAGE 36.

CYLINDERS.

Diameter of cylinders	12 inches.
Length of stroke	18 or 20 inches.

DRIVING-WHEELS.

Diameter of drivers	37 to 56 inches.

TRUCK.

FOUR-WHEELED CENTRE-BEARING TRUCK.

Diameter of wheels	20 to 28 inches.

WHEEL-BASE.

Total wheel-base	17 ft. 6 to 18 ft. 6
Rigid " (distance between driving-wheel centres) .	6 ft. 6 inches.

TENDER.

ON EIGHT WHEELS.

Capacity of tank	1500 gallons.

WEIGHT OF ENGINE IN WORKING ORDER.

On drivers	27,000 lbs.
On truck	17,000 "
Total weight of engine about . . .	44,000 "

LOAD.

IN ADDITION TO ENGINE AND TENDER.

130 lbs. initial pressure, cylinders 12x18—56 inch wheel		Cyls. 12x20. 37 in. wheel.	
Admission 50%.	70%	50%.	70%.
On a level . . . 514 .	670	883 .	1153
" 20 ft. grade . 229 .	304	404 .	533
" 40 " . . 123 .	188	251 .	334
" 60 " . 95 .	131	175 .	239
" 80 " . . 69 .	99	131 .	181
" 100 " . 52 .	76	112 .	154

CLASS P.

LOCOMOTIVE ENGINES FOR PASSENGER SERVICE.

GENERAL DESIGN ILLUSTRATED ON PAGE 41.

CYLINDERS.

Diameter of cylinders . . . . . . 13 inches.
Length of stroke . . . . . 20 or 22 inches.

DRIVING-WHEELS.

Diameter of wheels . . . . . . 54 to 66 inches.

TRUCK.

FOUR-WHEELED CENTRE-BEARING TRUCK.

Diameter of wheels . . . . . 26 to 30 inches.

WHEEL-BASE.

Total wheel-base . . . . . . 19 ft. 3 to 20 ft.
Rigid   "   (distance between driving-wheel centres) .   6 ft. 9 or 7 ft.

TENDER.

ON EIGHT WHEELS.

Capacity of tank . . . . 1500 gallons.

WEIGHT OF ENGINE IN WORKING ORDER.

On drivers . . . . 30,000 lbs.
On truck . . . . 20,000 "

Total weight of engine about . . . 50,000 "

LOAD.

IN ADDITION TO ENGINE AND TENDER.

130 lbs. initial pressure, cylinders 13x20—66 inch wheel		Cyls. 13x22. 54 in. wheel.	
Admission	50%. 70%.	50%.	70%.
On a level .	562 . . 741	811 .	. 1005
" 20 ft. grade	255 . 341	371 .	. 465
" 40 "	142 . . 208	225 .	. 292
" 60 "	104 . 146	161 .	. 201
" 80 "	78 . . 109	114 .	. 150
" 100 "	56 . 85	88 .	. 118

CLASS P.

LOCOMOTIVE ENGINES FOR PASSENGER SERVICE.

GENERAL DESIGN ILLUSTRATED ON PAGE 41.

CYLINDERS.

Diameter of cylinders . . . . . 14 inches.
Length of stroke . . . . . . 20 or 22 inches.

DRIVING-WHEELS.

Diameter of drivers . . . . 54 to 66 inches.

TRUCK.

FOUR-WHEELED CENTRE-BEARING TRUCK.

Diameter of wheels . . . . . 26 to 30 inches.

WHEEL-BASE.

Total wheel-base . . . . 20 ft. 2 to 20 ft. 9.
Rigid   "   (distance between driving-wheel centres) . 7 ft. to 7 ft. 3.

TENDER.

ON EIGHT WHEELS.

Capacity of tank . . . . 1500 gallons.

WEIGHT OF ENGINE IN WORKING ORDER.

On drivers . . . . 32,500 lbs
On truck . . . . 21,500 "
                                                    _____
Total weight of engine about . . . 54,000 "

LOAD.

IN ADDITION TO ENGINE AND TENDER.

130 lbs. initial pressure, cylinders 14x20—66 inch wheel		Cyls 14x22. 54 in. wheel.	
Admission . 50%. . 70%		50%. . .	70%.
On a level . . 654 . . 867		906 . .	1173
" 20 ft. grade . 300 . . 396		410 . .	537
" 40 " . . 184 . . 247		253 . .	337
" 60 " 127 . 174		176 . .	239
" 80 " . . 93 . . 130		131 . .	181
" 100 " . 71 . 102		101 . .	143

CLASS P.

LOCOMOTIVE ENGINES FOR PASSENGER SERVICE.

GENERAL DESIGN ILLUSTRATED ON PAGE 45.

CYLINDERS.

Diameter of cylinders . . . . . . 15 inches.
Length of stroke . . . . . . 20 "

DRIVING-WHEELS.

Diameter of drivers . . . . 54 to 66 inches.

TRUCK.

FOUR-WHEELED CENTRE-BEARING TRUCK.

Diameter of wheels . . . . . . 26 to 30 inches.

WHEEL-BASE.

Total wheel-base . . . . 20 ft. to 20 ft. 6.
Rigid   "   (distance between driving-wheel centres) . 7 ft. to 7 ft. 6.

TENDER.

ON EIGHT WHEELS.

Capacity of tank . . . . 1600 gallons.

WEIGHT OF ENGINE IN WORKING ORDER.

On drivers . . . . 35,000 lbs.
On truck . . . . 22,000 "
_____
Total weight of engine about . . . 57,000 "

LOAD.

IN ADDITION TO ENGINE AND TENDER.

130 lbs. initial pressure, cylinders 15x20—66 inch wheel		Cyls. 15x20. 54 in. wheel.	
Admission 50%. 70%.		50%.	70%.
On a level . . 765 . . 994		954	1234
" 20 ft. grade . 344 . . 454		434	569
" 40 " . . 211 . 283		270	359
" 60 " . 146 . 199		189	256
" 80 " . . 107 . 150		142	195
" 100 " . 82 . 117		111	155

CLASS P.

LOCOMOTIVE ENGINES FOR PASSENGER SERVICE

GENERAL DESIGN ILLUSTRATED ON PAGE 45.

CYLINDERS.

Diameter of cylinders	15 inches.
Length of stroke	22 and 24 inches.

DRIVING-WHEELS.

Diameter of drivers	54 to 66 inches.

TRUCK.

FOUR-WHEELED CENTRE-BEARING TRUCK.

Diameter of wheels	

WHEEL-BASE.

Total wheel-base	20 ft. 6 to 21 ft. 6.
Rigid " (distance between driving-wheel centres) .	7 ft. to 7 ft. 9.

TENDER.

ON EIGHT WHEELS.

Capacity of tank	1800 gallons.

WEIGHT OF ENGINE IN WORKING ORDER.

On drivers	36,000 lbs.
On truck	23,000 "
Total weight of engine about . . .	59,000 "

LOAD.

IN ADDITION TO ENGINE AND TENDER.

130 lbs. initial pressure, cylinders 15x22—66 inch wheel		Cyls. 15x24. 54 in. wheel.	
Admission . 50%. . 70%		50%. . .	70%.
On a level . . . 854 . . 1105		1148 . .	1469
" 20 ft. grade . 373 . 495		507 . .	668
" 40 " . . 239 . . 319		327 . .	433
" 60 " . 165 . 227		230 . .	309
" 80 " . . 124 . . 172		172 . .	235
" 100 " . 96 . 136		135 . .	187

CLASSES P. AND F.

LOCOMOTIVE ENGINES FOR PASSENGER OR FREIGHT SERVICE.

GENERAL DESIGN ILLUSTRATED ON PAGE 49.

CYLINDERS.

Diameter of cylinders	16 inches.
Length of stroke	20 "

DRIVING-WHEELS.

Diameter of drivers	48 inches.

TRUCK.
FOUR-WHEELED CENTRE-BEARING TRUCK.

Diameter of wheels	24 inches.

WHEEL-BASE.

Total wheel-base	21 ft. 3 to 21 ft. 6.
Rigid " (distance between driving-wheel centres) .	7 ft. 3 to 7 ft. 6.

TENDER.
ON EIGHT WHEELS.

Capacity of tank	1800 gallons.

WEIGHT OF ENGINE IN WORKING ORDER.

On drivers	36,000 lbs.
On truck	23,000 "
Total weight of engine about . . .	59,000 "

LOAD.
IN ADDITION TO ENGINE AND TENDER.

	16x20. 48 inch wheel	16x20. 48 in. wheel.
130 lbs. initial pressure, cylinders		
Admission	50%.	70%.
On a level	1240	1598
" 20 ft. grade	571	743
" 40 "	381	472
" 60 "	255	340
" 80 "	193	261
" 100 "	153	210

CLASSES P. AND F.

LOCOMOTIVE ENGINES FOR PASSENGER OR FREIGHT SERVICE.

GENERAL DESIGN ILLUSTRATED ON PAGE 49.

CYLINDERS.

Diameter of cylinders	16 inches.
Length of stroke	22 and 24 inches.

DRIVING-WHEELS.

Diameter of drivers	54 to 66 inches.

TRUCK.

FOUR-WHEELED CENTRE-BEARING TRUCK.

Diameter of wheels	26 to 30 inches.

WHEEL-BASE.

Total wheel-base	21 ft. 3 to 21 ft. 11.
Rigid " (distance between driving-wheel centres) .	7 ft. 6 to 8 ft.

TENDER.

ON EIGHT WHEELS.

Capacity of tank	1800 gallons.

WEIGHT OF ENGINE IN WORKING ORDER.

On drivers	40,000 lbs.
On truck	23,000 "
Total weight of engine about . . .	63,000 "

LOAD.

IN ADDITION TO ENGINE AND TENDER.

130 lbs. initial pressure, cylinders 16x22—66 inch wheel		Cyls. 16x24. 54 in. wheel.	
Admission 50%.	70%	50%.	70%.
On a level . . . 978 . . 1263		1315 . . 1730	
" 20 ft. grade . 446 . 583		604 . . 804	
" 40 " . . 277 . 368		377 . . 509	
" 60 " . 195 . 253		267 . . 365	
" 80 " . . 146 . 199		201 . . 280	
" 100 " . 114 . 159		159 . . 224	

CLASSES P. AND F.

LOCOMOTIVE ENGINES FOR PASSENGER OR FREIGHT SERVICE.

GENERAL DESIGN ILLUSTRATED ON PAGE 53.

CYLINDERS.

Diameter of cylinders . . . . . 17 inches.
Length of stroke . . . . 22 and 24 inches.

DRIVING-WHEELS.

Diameter of drivers . . . . 54 to 66 inches.

TRUCK.

FOUR-WHEELED CENTRE-BEARING TRUCK.

Diameter of wheels . . . . 26 to 30 inches.

WHEEL-BASE.

Total wheel-base . . . . 21 ft. 6 to 22 ft.
Rigid " (distance between driving-wheel centres) . 7 ft. 9 to 8 ft.

TENDER.

ON EIGHT WHEELS.

Capacity of tank . . . . 2000 gallons.

WEIGHT OF ENGINE IN WORKING ORDER.

On drivers . . . . . . 42,000 lbs.
On truck . . . . 24,000 "

Total weight of engine about . . . 66,000 "

LOAD.

IN ADDITION TO ENGINE AND TENDER.

130 lbs. initial pressure, cylinders 17x22—66 inch wheel		Cyls. 17x24. 54 in. wheel.	
Admission	50%.	70%	50%. 70%.
On a level . . . 1111 . . 1434		1477 . . 1909	
" 20 ft. grade . 513 . 673		692 . . 900	
" 40 " . . 317 . . 420		432 . . 564	
" 60 " . 225 . 301		307 . . 409	
" 80 " . . 169 . . 230		233 . . 314	
" 100 " . 133 . 184		184 . . 253	

CLASS M.

LOCOMOTIVE ENGINES FOR FREIGHT SERVICE.

GENERAL DESIGN ILLUSTRATED ON PAGE 56.

CYLINDERS.

Diameter of cylinders . . . . . 15 inches.

Length of stroke . . . . . . 24 "

DRIVING-WHEELS.

Rear and front pairs with flanged tires . . . 5¾ inches wide.

Intermediate pair with flat tires . . . . 6¼ " "

Diameter of drivers . . . . . . 45 to 49 inches.

TRUCK.

SINGLE PAIR OF TRUCK WHEELS IN RADIATING FRAME AND CONNECTED BY EQUALIZING LEVERS
WITH FRONT DRIVERS.

Diameter of wheels . . . . 30 inches.

WHEEL-BASE.

Total wheel-base . . . . . . 21 ft. 8½ inches.

Rigid " (distance bet. centres of rear and front drivers) 14 ft. 6 inches.

TENDER.
ON EIGHT WHEELS.

Capacity of tank . . . . . . 1800 gallons.

WEIGHT OF ENGINE IN WORKING ORDER.

On drivers . . . . 57,500 lbs.

On leading wheels . . . . . . 13,000 "

_____

Total weight of engine about . . . 70,500 "

LOAD.
IN ADDITION TO ENGINE AND TENDER.

130 lbs. initial pressure, cylinders 15x24—49 inch wheel		Cyls. 15x24. 45 in. wheel.	
Admission 50%.	70%.	50%.	70%.
On a level . 1270	1640	1392	1795
" 20 ft. grade 582	759	648	834
" 40 " 364	481	403	530
" 60 " 260	345	287	382
" 80 " 194	264	220	293
" 100 " 153	211	172	235

CLASS M.

LOCOMOTIVE ENGINES FOR FREIGHT SERVICE.

GENERAL DESIGN ILLUSTRATED ON PAGE 56.

CYLINDERS.

Diameter of cylinders . . . . . . 15 inches.
Length of stroke . . . . . . 24 "

DRIVING-WHEELS.

Rear and front pairs with flanged tires . . . 5¾ inches wide.
Intermediate pair with flat tires . . . . 6¼ " "
Diameter of drivers . . . . . . 56 inches.

TRUCK.

SINGLE PAIR OF TRUCK WHEELS IN RADIATING FRAME AND CONNECTED BY EQUALIZING LEVERS
WITH FRONT DRIVERS.

Diameter of wheels . . . . . . 30 to 33 inches.

WHEEL-BASE.

Total wheel-base . . . . . . 21 ft. 10 inches.
Rigid " (distance bet. centres of rear and front drivers) 14 ft. 6 inches.

TENDER.

ON EIGHT WHEELS.

Capacity of tank . . . . . . 1800 gallons.

WEIGHT OF ENGINE IN WORKING ORDER.

On drivers . . . . 57,500 lbs.
On leading wheels . . . . . . 13,000 "
                                                        ————
Total weight of engine about . . . 70,500 "

LOAD.

IN ADDITION TO ENGINE AND TENDER.

130 lbs. initial pressure, cylinders 15x24—56 inch wheel	Cyls. 15x24. 56 in. wheel.
Admission . . . . 50%.	. . 70%.
On a level 1098	. . 1422
" 20 ft. grade 499	. . 655
" 40 " 310	. . 412
" 60 " 217	. . 299
" 80 " 162	. . 223
" 100 " 126	. . 177

CLASS M.

LOCOMOTIVE ENGINES FOR FREIGHT SERVICE.

GENERAL DESIGN ILLUSTRATED ON PAGE 56.

CYLINDERS.

Diameter of cylinders . . . . . . 16 inches.
Length of stroke . . . . . 22 or 24 inches.

DRIVING-WHEELS.

Rear and front pairs with flanged tires . . . 5¾ inches wide.
Intermediate pair with flat tires . . . . 6¼ " "
Diameter of drivers . . . . . 45 to 49 inches.

TRUCK.

SINGLE PAIR OF TRUCK WHEELS IN RADIATING FRAME AND CONNECTED BY EQUALIZING LEVERS
WITH FRONT DRIVERS.

Diameter of wheels . . . . 30 inches.

WHEEL-BASE.

Total wheel-base . . . . . 21 ft. 2½ to 21 ft. 6½ inches.
Rigid " (distance bet. centres of rear and front drivers)

14 ft. 2 to 14 ft. 6 inches.

TENDER.

ON EIGHT WHEELS.

Capacity of tank . . . . 1800 gallons.

WEIGHT OF ENGINE IN WORKING ORDER.

On drivers . . . . 57,500 lbs.
On leading wheels . . . . . . 14,000 "

Total weight of engine about . . . 71,500 "

LOAD.

IN ADDITION TO ENGINE AND TENDER.

130 lbs. initial pressure, cylinders 16x22—49 inch wheel | Cyls. 16x24. 45 in. wheel.

	Admission	50%.		70%.	50%.			70%.
On a level	.	1374	.	1722	1592	.	.	2087
" 20 ft. grade	.	616	.	802	732	.	.	970
" 40 "	.	388	.	510	461	.	.	618
" 60 "	.	276	.	367	328	.	.	445
" 80 "	.	210	.	283	249	.	.	342
" 100 "	.	167	.	228	198	.	.	276

CLASS M.

LOCOMOTIVE ENGINES FOR FREIGHT SERVICE.

GENERAL DESIGN ILLUSTRATED ON PAGE 56.

CYLINDERS.

Diameter of cylinders	16 inches.
Length of stroke	22 or 24 inches.

DRIVING-WHEELS.

Rear and front pairs with flanged tires . . .	5¾ inches wide.
Intermediate pair with flat tires	6¼ " "
Diameter of drivers	56 inches.

TRUCK.

SINGLE PAIR OF TRUCK WHEELS IN RADIATING FRAME AND CONNECTED BY EQUALIZING LEVERS WITH FRONT DRIVERS.

Diameter of wheels	30 or 33 inches.

WHEEL-BASE.

Total wheel-base	21 ft. 8 to 22 ft.
Rigid " (distance bet. centres of rear and front drivers)	
	14 ft. 2 to 14 ft. 6 inches.

TENDER.

ON EIGHT WHEELS.

Capacity of tank	1800 gallons.

WEIGHT OF ENGINE IN WORKING ORDER.

On drivers	58,000 lbs.
On leading wheels ·	14,000 "
Total weight of engine about . . .	72,000 "

LOAD.

IN ADDITION TO ENGINE AND TENDER.

130 lbs. initial pressure, cylinders 16x22—56 inch wheel		Cyls. 16x24. 56 in. wheel.	
Admission	50%.	70%	50%.	70%
On a level	1156	1495	1252	1652
" 20 ft. grade	529	692	567	761
" 40 "	331	438	358	481
" 60 "	234	313	248	342
" 80 "	176	240	186	260
" 100 "	139	193	146	207

CLASS M.

LOCOMOTIVE ENGINES FOR FREIGHT SERVICE.

GENERAL DESIGN ILLUSTRATED ON PAGE 62.

CYLINDERS.

Diameter of cylinders . . . . . . 17 inches.
Length of stroke . . . . . . 22 or 24 inches.

DRIVING-WHEELS.

Rear and front pairs with flanged tires . . . 5¾ inches wide.
Intermediate pair with flat tires . . . 6¼ " "
Diameter of drivers . . . . . 45 to 49 inches.

TRUCK.

SINGLE PAIR OF TRUCK WHEELS IN RADIATING FRAME AND CONNECTED BY EQUALIZING LEVERS WITH FRONT DRIVERS.

Diameter of wheels . . . . . . 30 inches.

WHEEL-BASE.

Total wheel-base . . . . 21 ft. to 22 ft.
Rigid " (distance bet. centres of rear and front drivers)
14 ft. to 14 ft. 10 inches.

TENDER.

ON EIGHT WHEELS.

Capacity of tank . . . . 1800 gallons.

WEIGHT OF ENGINE IN WORKING ORDER.

On drivers . . . . 59,000 lbs.
On leading wheels . . . . . . 14,000 "

Total weight of engine about . . 73,000 "

LOAD.

IN ADDITION TO ENGINE AND TENDER.

130 lbs. initial pressure, cylinders 17x22—49 inch wheel			Cyls. 17x24. 45 in. wheel.		
Admission	50%.	70%.	50%.		70%.
On a level	1519	1954	1805		2323
" 20 ft. grade	703	912	835		1084
" 40 "	404	582	529		692
" 60 "	318	421	378		500
" 80 "	244	326	289		387
" 100 "	196	263	231		313

CLASS M.

LOCOMOTIVE ENGINES FOR FREIGHT SERVICE.

GENERAL DESIGN ILLUSTRATED ON PAGE 62.

CYLINDERS.

Diameter of cylinders	17 inches.
Length of stroke	22 or 24 inches.

DRIVING-WHEELS.

Rear and front pairs with flanged tires . . .	5¾ inches wide.
Intermediate pair with flat tires	6¼ " "
Diameter of drivers	56 inches.

TRUCK.

SINGLE PAIR OF TRUCK WHEELS IN RADIATING FRAME AND CONNECTED BY EQUALIZING LEVERS WITH FRONT DRIVERS.

Diameter of wheels	30 to 33 inches.

WHEEL-BASE.

Total wheel-base	21 ft. 6 to 22 ft. 4 inches.
Rigid " (distance bet. centres of rear and front drivers)	
	14 ft. to 14 ft. 10 inches.

TENDER.

ON EIGHT WHEELS.

Capacity of tank	1800 gallons.

WEIGHT OF ENGINE IN WORKING ORDER.

On drivers	59,000 lbs.
On leading wheels	14,000 "
Total weight of engine about . . .	73,000 "

LOAD.

IN ADDITION TO ENGINE AND TENDER.

130 lbs. initial pressure, cylinders 17x22—56 inch wheel		Cyls. 17x24. 56 in. wheel.	
Admission 50%. 70%		50%. 70%	
On a level . . . 1317 . 1697		1427 . . 1843	
" 20 ft. grade . 606 . 790		653 . . 853	
" 40 " . 382 . . 502		409 . . 541	
" 60 " . 272 . 362		289 . . 387	
" 80 " . 206 . . 278		218 . . 296	
" 100 " . 164 . 223		172 . . 237	

CLASS M.

LOCOMOTIVE ENGINES FOR FREIGHT SERVICE.

GENERAL DESIGN ILLUSTRATED ON PAGE 62.

CYLINDERS.

Diameter of cylinders . . . . . 18 inches.
Length of stroke . . . . . 22 or 24 inches.

DRIVING-WHEELS.

Rear and front pairs with flanged tires . . . 5¾ inches wide.
Intermediate pair with flat tires . . . . . 6¼ " "
Diameter of drivers . . . . . . 45 to 49 inches.

TRUCK.

SINGLE PAIR OF TRUCK WHEELS IN RADIATING FRAME AND CONNECTED BY EQUALIZING LEVERS
WITH FRONT DRIVERS.

Diameter of wheels . . . . . . 30 inches.

WHEEL-BASE.

Total wheel-base . . . . . . 21 ft. to 22 ft. 2 inches.
Rigid " (distance bet. centres of rear and front drivers)
                                                14 ft. to 15 ft.

TENDER.

ON EIGHT WHEELS.

Capacity of tank . . . . 2000 gallons.

WEIGHT OF ENGINE IN WORKING ORDER.

On drivers . . . . 61,500 lbs.
On leading wheels . . . . . . 14,000 "
                                      _____
Total weight of engine about . . . 75,500 "

LOAD.

IN ADDITION TO ENGINE AND TENDER.

130 lbs. initial pressure, cylinders 18x22—49 inch wheel			Cyls. 18x24. 45 in. wheel.		
Admission	50%.	70%	50%.		70%.
On a level	1728	2217	2055		2340
" 20 ft. grade	801	1030	952		1088
" 40 "	507	662	603		693
" 60 "	354	479	432		499
" 80 "	279	371	330		385
" 100 "	223	300	265		309

CLASS M.

LOCOMOTIVE ENGINES FOR FREIGHT SERVICE.

GENERAL DESIGN ILLUSTRATED ON PAGE 62.

CYLINDERS.

Diameter of cylinders	18 inches.
Length of stroke	22 or 24 inches.

DRIVING-WHEELS.

Rear and front pairs with flanged tires . . .	5¾ inches wide.
Intermediate pair with flat tires	6¼ " "
Diameter of drivers	56 inches.

TRUCK.

SINGLE PAIR OF TRUCK WHEELS IN RADIATING FRAME AND CONNECTED BY EQUALIZING LEVERS
WITH FRONT DRIVERS.

Diameter of wheels	30 or 33 inches.

WHEEL-BASE.

Total wheel-base	21 ft. 6 to 22 ft. 6 inches.
Rigid " (distance bet. centres of rear and front drivers)	
	14 ft. to 15 ft.

TENDER.

ON EIGHT WHEELS.

Capacity of tank	2000 gallons.

WEIGHT OF ENGINE IN WORKING ORDER.

On drivers	61,500 lbs.
On leading wheels	14,500 "
Total weight of engine about . . .	76,000 "

LOAD.

IN ADDITION TO ENGINE AND TENDER.

130 lbs. initial pressure, cylinders 18x22—56 inch wheel		Cyls. 18x24. 56 in. wheel.	
Admission . 50%. . 70%		50%. . .	70%.
On a level . . . 1484 . . 1911		1608 . .	2075
" 20 ft. grade . 692 . 891		739 . .	963
" 40 " . 432 . . 568		462 . .	612
" 60 " . 309 . 409		328 . .	439
" 80 " . 235 . . 316		249 . .	338
" 100 " . 188 . 254		198 . .	271

CLASS S.

SWITCHING ENGINES WITH SEPARATE TENDER.

GENERAL DESIGN ILLUSTRATED ON PAGE 68.

CYLINDERS.

Diameter of cylinders . . . . 13 inches.

Length of stroke . . . . 22 "

DRIVING-WHEELS.

Diameter of drivers . . . . . . 42 to 49 inches.

Distance between centre, (4) . . . . . 6 ft. 9 inches.

TENDER.

On four to eight wheels . . . . . 26 inches Diameter.

Capacity of tank . . . . . . 800 to 1500 gallons.

WEIGHT OF ENGINE IN WORKING ORDER.

Total weight of engine about . . . . . 36,000 lbs.

LOAD.

IN ADDITION TO ENGINE AND TENDER.

130 lbs. initial pressure, cylinders 13x22—49 inch wheel			Cyls. 13x22. 42 in. wheel.		
Admission	50%.	70%.	50%.		70%.
On a level	874	1140	1031		1340
" 20 ft. grade	401	522	476		624
" 40 "	252	336	301		399
" 60 "	179	241	215		288
" 80 "	135	185	164		222
" 100 "	107	149	132		180

CLASS S.

SWITCHING ENGINES WITH SEPARATE TENDER.

GENERAL DESIGN ILLUSTRATED ON PAGE 68.

CYLINDERS.

Diameter of cylinders	14 inches.
Length of stroke	22 "

DRIVING-WHEELS.

Diameter of drivers	42 to 49 inches.
Distance between centres, (4)	7 feet.

TENDER.

On four to eight wheels	26 inches Diameter.
Capacity of tank	800 to 1600 gallons.

WEIGHT OF ENGINE IN WORKING ORDER.

Total weight of engine about	40,000 lbs.

LOAD.

IN ADDITION TO ENGINE AND TENDER.

130 lbs. initial pressure, cylinders 14x22—49 inch wheel		Cyls. 14x22. 42 in. wheel.	
Admission . 50%. . . 70%.		50%. . . 70%.	
On a level . . 1031 . . 1339		1211 . . 1556	
" 20 ft. grade . 474 . 616		562 . . 721	
" 40 " . . 299 . . 392		356 . . 465	
" 60 " . 213 . 283		256 . . 337	
" 80 " . 162 . . 217		196 . . 261	
" 100 " . 129 . 178		158 . . 212	

CLASS S.

SWITCHING ENGINES WITH SEPARATE TENDER.

GENERAL DESIGN ILLUSTRATED ON PAGE 68.

CYLINDERS.

Diameter of cylinders . . . . 15 inches.

Length of stroke . . . . 22 "

DRIVING-WHEELS.

Diameter of drivers . . . . . . 42 to 49 inches.

Distance between centres, (4) . . . . . . 7 feet.

TENDER.

On four to eight wheels . . . . 26 inches Diameter.

Capacity of tank . . . . 1000 to 1800 gallons.

WEIGHT OF ENGINE IN WORKING ORDER.

Total weight of engine about . . . . . 46,000 lbs.

LOAD.

IN ADDITION TO ENGINE AND TENDER.

130 lbs. initial pressure, cylinders 15x22—49 inch wheel		Cyls. 15x22. 42 in. wheel.	
Admission	50%. 70%	50%.	70%.
On a level	1185 . 1522	1392 .	1788
" 20 ft. grade	546 . 709	647 .	837
" 40 "	345 . 452	411 .	536
" 60 "	246 . 326	295 .	389
" 80 "	788 . 251	227 .	301
" 100 "	150 . 203	183 .	267

CLASS S.

SWITCHING ENGINES WITH SEPARATE TENDER.

GENERAL DESIGN ILLUSTRATED ON PAGE 68.

CYLINDERS.

Diameter of cylinders	16 inches.
Length of stroke	22 "

DRIVING-WHEELS.

Diameter of drivers	42 to 49 inches.
Distance between centres, (4)	7 feet.

TENDER.

On four to eight wheels	26 inches Diameter.
Capacity of tank	1000 to 1800 gallons.

WEIGHT OF ENGINE IN WORKING ORDER.

Total weight of engine about	50,000 lbs.

LOAD.

IN ADDITION TO ENGINE AND TENDER.

130 lbs. initial pressure, cylinders 16x22—49 inch wheel		Cyls. 16x22. 42 in. wheel.	
Admission . 50%.	70%.	50%. .	70%.
On a level . . . 1352 .	1771	1589 . .	2079
" 20 ft. grade . 627 .	821	740 . .	976
" 40 " . . 397 . .	529	472 .	626
" 60 " . 283 .	382	339 . .	455
" 80 " . . 217 . .	296	262 . .	354
" 100 " . 174 .	240	212 . .	288

CLASS S.

SWITCHING ENGINES WITH SEPARATE TENDER.

GENERAL DESIGN ILLUSTRATED ON PAGE 74.

CYLINDERS.

Diameter of cylinders . . . . 15 inches.

Length of stroke . . . . 22 "

DRIVING-WHEELS.

Diameter of drivers . . . . . . 42 to 49 inches.

Distance between centres, (6) . . . . . 10 ft. 3 inches.

TENDER.

On four to eight wheels . . . . . 26 inches Diameter.

Capacity of tank . . . . . . 1000 to 1800 gallons.

WEIGHT OF ENGINE IN WORKING ORDER.

Total weight of engine about . . . . 58,000 lbs.

LOAD.

IN ADDITION TO ENGINE AND TENDER.

130 lbs. initial pressure, cylinders 15x22—49 inch wheel		Cyls. 15x22. 42 in. wheel.	
Admission 50%. 70%		50%.	70%.
On a level 1027 1509		1377	1774
" 20 ft. grade 537 699		637	820
" 40 " 336 443		402	527
" 60 " 238 318		288	381
" 80 " 180 244		219	293
" 100 " 143 196		175	237

CLASS S.

SWITCHING ENGINES WITH SEPARATE TENDER.

GENERAL DESIGN ILLUSTRATED ON PAGE 74.

CYLINDERS.

Diameter of cylinders	16 inches.
Length of stroke	22 "

DRIVING-WHEELS.

Diameter of drivers	42 to 49 inches.
Distance between centres, (6)	10 ft. 5 inches.

TENDER.

On four to eight wheels	26 inches Diameter.
Capacity of tank	1000 to 1800 gallons.

WEIGHT OF ENGINE IN WORKING ORDER.

Total weight of engine about	60,000 lbs.

LOAD.

IN ADDITION TO ENGINE AND TENDER.

130 lbs. initial pressure, cylinders 16x22—49 inch wheel		Cyls. 16x22. 42 in. wheel.	
Admission 50%.	70%.	50%.	70%.
On a level 1340	1760	1578	2068
" 20 ft. grade 618	819	732	967
" 40 " 390	522	465	619
" 60 " 278	377	334	449
" 80 " 211	290	256	348
" 100 " 168	212	206	282

CLASS S.

SWITCHING ENGINES WITH SEPARATE TENDER.

GENERAL DESIGN ILLUSTRATED ON PAGE 74.

CYLINDERS.

Diameter of cylinders . . . . 17 inches.

Length of stroke . . . . 22 "

DRIVING-WHEELS.

Diameter of drivers . . . . . . 42 to 49 inches.

Distance between centres, (6) . . . . . 10 ft. 7 inches.

TENDER.

On four to eight wheels . . . . . 26 inches Diameter.

Capacity of tank . . . . . . 1000 to 2000 gallons.

WEIGHT OF ENGINE IN WORKING ORDER.

Total weight of engine about . . . . 64,000 lbs.

LOAD.

IN ADDITION TO ENGINE AND TENDER.

130 lbs. initial pressure, cylinders 17x22—49 inch wheel			Cyls. 17x22. 42 in. wheel.	
Admission	50%.	70%	50%.	70%
On a level . . .	1519 .	. 1955	1788 .	2296
" 20 ft. grade .	702	. 912	832 .	1075
" 40 " .	. 444	. 582	529	. 689
" 60 " .	318	. 420	381	500
" 80 " .	. 242	. 324	293 .	. 388
" 100 " .	194	. 262	236 .	. 315

CLASS S. T.

SWITCHING TANK ENGINES.

GENERAL DESIGN ILLUSTRATED ON PAGE 79.

CYLINDERS.

Diameter of cylinders	9 inches.
Length of stroke	16 "

DRIVING-WHEELS.

Diameter of drivers	30¼ to 49 inches.
Distance between centres, (4)	6 ft. 3 inches.

TANK.

Capacity of tank	300 to 400 gallons.

WEIGHT OF ENGINE IN WORKING ORDER.

Total weight of engine about	24,000 lbs.

LOAD.

IN ADDITION TO ENGINE AND TENDER.

130 lbs. initial pressure, cylinders 9x16—49 inch wheel		Cyls. 9x16. 30¼ in. wheel.	
Admission 50%.	70%.	50%.	70%.
On a level 301	390	505	650
" 20 ft. grade 138	181	236	305
" 40 " 86	114	151	196
" 60 " 61	82	109	143
" 80 ' 46	63	85	112
" 100 ' 37	51	69	92

CLASS S. T.

SWITCHING TANK ENGINES.

GENERAL DESIGN ILLUSTRATED ON PAGE 79.

CYLINDERS.

Diameter of cylinders . . . . 10 inches.

Length of stroke . . . . 16 "

DRIVING-WHEELS.

Diameter of drivers . . . . . . $30\frac{1}{4}$ to 49 inches.

Distance between centres, (4) . . . . . 6 ft. 3 inches.

TANK.

Capacity of tank . . . . . . 300 to 400 gallons.

WEIGHT OF ENGINE IN WORKING ORDER.

Total weight of engine about . . . 26,000 lbs.

LOAD.

IN ADDITION TO ENGINE AND TENDER.

130 lbs. initial pressure, cylinders 10x16—49 inch wheel		Cyls. 10x16. $30\frac{1}{4}$ in. wheel.	
Admission . 50%. . 70%		50%. . .	70%.
On a level . . . 376 . . 485		628 . .	805
" 20 ft. grade . 173 . . 226		294 . .	380
" 40 " . . 109 . . 144		189 . .	245
" 60 " . 78 . 104		137 . .	179
" 80 " . . 59 . . 80		107 . .	140
" 100 " . 48 . . 65		87 .	115

CLASS S. T.

SWITCHING TANK ENGINES.

GENERAL DESIGN ILLUSTRATED ON PAGE 79.

CYLINDERS.

Diameter of cylinders	10½ inches.
Length of stroke	18 "

DRIVING-WHEELS.

Diameter of drivers	30¼ to 49 inches.
Distance between centres, (4)	6 ft. 6 inches.

TANK.

Capacity of tank	350 to 450 gallons.

WEIGHT OF ENGINE IN WORKING ORDER.

Total weight of engine about	30,000 lbs.

LOAD.

IN ADDITION TO ENGINE AND TENDER.

130 lbs. initial pressure, cylinders 10½x18—49 in. wheel Cyls.10½x18. 30¼ in.wheel

	50%.	70%.	50%.	70%.
Admission	50%.	70%.	50%.	70%.
On a level . . .	470	605	781 . .	1004
" 20 ft. grade .	217	282	374 . .	474
" 40 " . .	138	180	236 . .	306
" 60 " .	99	130	172 . .	224
" 80 " . .	75	101	134 . .	176
" 100 " .	61	82	110 . .	145

CLASS S. T.

SWITCHING TANK ENGINES.

GENERAL DESIGN ILLUSTRATED ON PAGE 79.

CYLINDERS.

Diameter of cylinders . . . . 11 inches.

Length of stroke . . . . . . 18 or 20 "

DRIVING-WHEELS.

Diameter of drivers . . . . . . 37 to 49 inches.

Distance between centres, (4) . . . . . 6 ft. 6 inches.

TANK.

Capacity of tank . . . . . . 400 to 500 gallons.

WEIGHT OF ENGINE IN WORKING ORDER.

Total weight of engine about . . . 36,000 lbs.

LOAD.

IN ADDITION TO ENGINE AND TENDER.

130 lbs. initial pressure, cylinders 11x18—49 inch wheel		Cyls. 11x20. 37 in. wheel.	
Admission 50%. 70%		50%.	70%.
On a level 515 . . 665		767 . .	1003
" 20 ft. grade 239 311		357 . .	463
" 40 " 152 . . 198		227 . .	297
" 60 " 109 144		164 .	216
" 80 " 83 . . 111		126 . .	167
" 100 " 67 90		103 . .	137

CLASS S. T.

SWITCHING TANK ENGINES.

GENERAL DESIGN ILLUSTRATED ON PAGE 79.

CYLINDERS.

Diameter of cylinders . . . . . . 12 inches.
Length of stroke . . . . . . 18 or 20 "

DRIVING-WHEELS.

Diameter of drivers . . . . . 37 to 49 inches.
Distance between centres, (4) . . . . . 6 ft. 6 inches.

TANK.

Capacity of tank . . . . . . 450 to 600 gallons.

WEIGHT OF ENGINE IN WORKING ORDER.

Total weight of engine about . . . . . 40,000 lbs.

LOAD.

IN ADDITION TO ENGINE AND TENDER.

130 lbs. initial pressure, cylinders 12x18—49 in. wheel		Cyls. 12x20. 37 in. wheel	
Admission . 50%. . 70%.		50%. . . 70%.	
On a level . . . 616 . . 794		916 . . 1177	
" 20 ft. grade . 287 . 372		429 . . 554	
" 40 " . . 182 . 238		274 . . 356	
" 60 " . 131 . 173		198 . . 260	
" 80 " . . 101 . 135		153 . . 202	
" 100 " . 81 . 109		124 . . 165	

CLASS S. T.

SWITCHING TANK ENGINES.

GENERAL DESIGN ILLUSTRATED ON PAGE 79.

CYLINDERS.

Diameter of cylinders . . . . 13 inches.

Length of stroke . . . . . . 20 or 22 "

DRIVING-WHEELS.

Diameter of drivers . . . . . 37 to 49 inches.

Distance between centres, (4) . . . . . 6 ft. 9 inches.

TANK.

Capacity of tank . . . . . . 500 to 600 gallons.

WEIGHT OF ENGINE IN WORKING ORDER.

Total weight of engine about . . . 45,000 lbs.

LOAD.

IN ADDITION TO ENGINE AND TENDER.

130 lbs. initial pressure, cylinders 13x20—49 inch wheel		Cyls. 13x22. 37 in. wheel.	
Admission	50%.	70%	50%.	70%.
On a level	800	1042	1192	1530
" 20 ft. grade	374	489	559	721
" 40 "	239	315	359	466
" 60 "	173	229	261	341
" 80 "	133	179	203	266
" 100 "	109	147	166	218

CLASS S. T.

SWITCHING TANK ENGINES.

GENERAL DESIGN ILLUSTRATED ON PAGE 79.

CYLINDERS.

Diameter of cylinders	14 inches.
Length of stroke	22 "

DRIVING-WHEELS.

Diameter of drivers	37 to 49 inches.
Distance between centres, (4)	7 feet.

TANK.

Capacity of tank	600 gallons.

WEIGHT OF ENGINE IN WORKING ORDER.

Total weight of engine about	50,000 lbs.

LOAD.

IN ADDITION TO ENGINE AND TENDER.

130 lbs. initial pressure, cylinders 14x22—49 in. wheel		Cyls. 14x22. 37 in. wheel	
Admission . 50%. .	70%.	50%. . .	70%
On a level . . . 1036 . .	1331	1392 . .	1783
" 20 ft. grade . 484 .	627	655 . .	843
" 40 " . . 310 . .	403	422 . .	546
" 60 " . 224 .	294	308 . .	400
" 80 " . . 174 .	229	240 . .	314
" 100 " . 141 .	188	197 . .	258

CLASS S. T.

SWITCHING TANK ENGINES.

GENERAL DESIGN ILLUSTRATED ON PAGE 79.

CYLINDERS.

Diameter of cylinders . . . . 15 inches.

Length of stroke . . . . 22 "

DRIVING-WHEELS.

Diameter of drivers . . . . . . 37 to 49 inches.

Distance between centres, (4) . . . . . . 7 feet.

TANK.

Capacity of tank . . . . 600 gallons.

WEIGHT OF ENGINE IN WORKING ORDER.

Total weight of engine about . . . 55,000 lbs.

LOAD.

IN ADDITION TO ENGINE AND TENDER.

130 lbs. initial pressure, cylinders 15x22—49 inch wheel		Cyls. 15x22. 37 in. wheel.	
Admission . 50%. . 70%		50%. . .	70%.
On a level . . . 1192 . . 1531		1600 .	. 2050
" 20 ft. grade . 558 . . 721		754 . .	970
" 40 " . . 357 . . 465		486 . .	628
" 60 " . 263 . . 342		359 . .	465
" 80 " . . 201 . . 265		278 . .	362
" 100 " . 164 . . 217		228 . .	298

CLASS S. T.

SWITCHING TANK ENGINES.

GENERAL DESIGN ILLUSTRATED ON PAGE 89.

CYLINDERS.

Diameter of cylinders	15 inches.
Length of stroke	22 "

DRIVING-WHEELS.

Diameter of drivers	37 to 49 inches.
Distance between centres, (6)	10 ft. 3 inches.

TANK.

Capacity of tank	600 to 700 gallons.

WEIGHT OF ENGINE IN WORKING ORDER.

Total weight of engine about	60,000 lbs.

LOAD.

IN ADDITION TO ENGINE AND TENDER.

130 lbs. initial pressure, cylinders 15x22—49 in. wheel		Cyls. 15x22. 37 in. wheel	
Admission 50%.	70%.	50%.	70%.
On a level . . . 1192	1531	1600	2050
" 20 ft. grade . 558	721	754	970
" 40 " . 357	465	486	628
" 60 " . 263	342	359	465
" 80 " . 201	265	278	362
" 100 " . 164	217	228	298

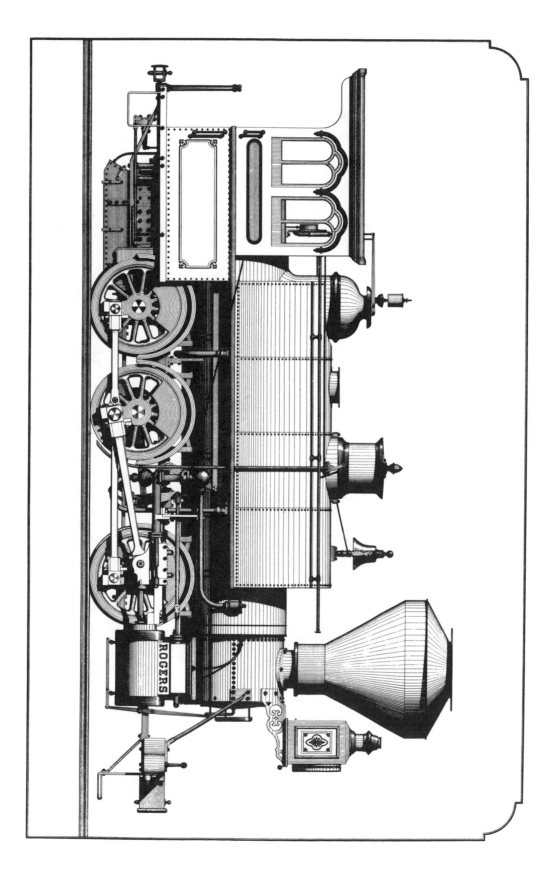

CLASS S. T.

SWITCHING TANK ENGINES.

GENERAL DESIGN ILLUSTRATED ON PAGE 89.

CYLINDERS.

Diameter of cylinders . . . . 16 inches.

Length of stroke . . . . 22 "

DRIVING-WHEELS.

Diameter of drivers . . . . . . 37 to 49 inches.

Distance between centres, (6) . . . . . 10 ft. 5 inches.

TANK.

Capacity of tank . . . . 700 gallons.

WEIGHT OF ENGINE IN WORKING ORDER.

Total weight of engine about . . . 64,000 lbs.

LOAD.

IN ADDITION TO ENGINE AND TENDER.

130 lbs. initial pressure, cylinders 16x22—49 inch wheel		Cyls. 16x22. 37 in. wheel.	
Admission . 50%. . 70%		50%. . .	70%.
On a level . . . 1355 . . 1774		1820 . .	2375
" 20 ft. grade . 634 . 835		857 . .	1124
" 40 " . . 406 . . 538		558 . .	728
" 60 " . 297 . 396		407 . .	538
" 80 " . . 228 . . 306		315 . .	419
" 100 " . 185 . 251		258 . .	345

CLASS T. W.

TEN WHEELED LOCOMOTIVE ENGINES, FREIGHT SERVICE.

GENERAL DESIGN ILLUSTRATED ON PAGE 93.

CYLINDERS.

Diameter of cylinders	15 inches.
Length of stroke	22 or 24 "

DRIVING-WHEELS.

Rear and middle pair with flanged tires	5¾ inches wide.
Front pair with flat tires	6¼ " "
Diameter of drivers	48 to 56 inches.

TRUCK.

FOUR WHEELED RADIATING TRUCK.

Diameter of wheels	24 to 28 inches.

WHEEL-BASE.

Total wheel-base	21 ft. 2 inches to 22 ft.
Distance between centres of front and rear drivers	12 ft. to 12 ft. 6 inches.

TENDER.

ON EIGHT WHEELS.

Capacity of tank	1800 gallons.

WEIGHT OF ENGINE IN WORKING ORDER.

On drivers	49,000 lbs.
On truck	19,000 "
Total weight of engine about	68,000 lbs.

LOAD.

IN ADDITION TO ENGINE AND TENDER.

130 lbs. initial pressure, cylinders 15x22—56 in. wheel		Cyls. 15x24. 48 in. wheel	
Admission	50%.	70%.	50%.	70%.
On a level	918	1307	1293	1671
" 20 ft. grade	460	603	591	772
" 40 "	285	380	367	487
" 60 "	200	271	259	349
" 80 "	150	206	195	266
" 100 "	118	164	151	215

CLASS T. W.

TEN WHEELED LOCOMOTIVE ENGINES, FREIGHT SERVICE.

GENERAL DESIGN ILLUSTRATED ON PAGE 93.

CYLINDERS.

Diameter of cylinders . . . . . . 16 inches.

Length of stroke . . . . . 22 or 24 "

DRIVING-WHEELS.

Rear and middle pair with flanged tires . . . 5¾ inches wide.

Front pair with flat tires . . . . . 6¼ " "

Diameter of drivers . . . . . 48 to 56 inches.

TRUCK.

FOUR WHEELED RADIATING TRUCK.

Diameter of wheels . . . . . . 24 to 28 inches.

WHEEL-BASE.

Total wheel-base . . . . . 21 ft. 2 in. to 22 ft. 3 inches.

Distance between centres of front and rear drivers . 12 ft. to 12 ft. 8 inches.

TENDER.

ON EIGHT WHEELS.

Capacity of tank . . . . . . 1800 gallons.

WEIGHT OF ENGINE IN WORKING ORDER.

On drivers . . . . 50,500 lbs.

On truck . . . . 20,000 "

Total weight of engine about . . . . . 70,500 lbs.

LOAD.

IN ADDITION TO ENGINE AND TENDER.

130 lbs. initial pressure, cylinders 16x22—56 inch wheel		Cyls. 16x24. 48 in. wheel.	
Admission	50%.	70%	50%.	70%.
On a level	1158	1496	1499	1950
" 20 ft. grade	530	692	680	905
" 40 "	336	439	427	570
" 60 "	235	314	303	413
" 80 "	177	241	230	317
" 100 "	140	193	182	255

CLASS T. W.

TEN WHEELED LOCOMOTIVE ENGINES, FREIGHT SERVICE.

GENERAL DESIGN ILLUSTRATED ON PAGE 97.

CYLINDERS.

Diameter of cylinders . . . . 17 inches.
Length of stroke . . . . . . 22 or 24 "

DRIVING-WHEELS.

Rear and middle pair with flanged tires . . . 5¾ inches wide.
Front pair with flat tires . . . . . . 6¼ " "
Diameter of drivers . . . . . 48 to 56 inches.

TRUCK.

FOUR WHEELED RADIATING TRUCK.

Diameter of wheels . . . . 24 to 28 inches.

WHEEL-BASE.

Total wheel-base . . . . 21 ft. 5 inches to 23 ft.
Distance between centres of front and rear drivers . 12 ft. to 13 ft. 2 inches.

TENDER.

ON EIGHT WHEELS.

Capacity of tank . . . . 2000 gallons.

WEIGHT OF ENGINE IN WORKING ORDER.

On drivers . . . . 52,500 lbs.
On truck . . . . 20,500 "
Total weight of engine about . . . . 73,000 lbs.

LOAD.

IN ADDITION TO ENGINE AND TENDER.

130 lbs. initial pressure, cylinders 17x22—56 in. wheel		Cyls. 17x24. 48 in. wheel.	
Admission . 50%.	70%.	50%.	70%.
On a level . . 1316 .	1697	1684 . .	2122
" 20 ft. grade . 605 .	788	776 . .	1010
" 40 " . 381 .	501	489 .	642
" 60 " . 270	360	349 . .	463
" 80 " . 205 .	276	265 . .	356
" 100 " . 163	222	211 . .	288

CLASS T. W.

TEN WHEELED LOCOMOTIVE ENGINES, FREIGHT SERVICE

GENERAL DESIGN ILLUSTRATED ON PAGE 97.

CYLINDERS.

Diameter of cylinders	18 inches.
Length of stroke	22 or 24 "

DRIVING-WHEELS.

Rear and middle pair with flanged tires . . .	5¾ inches wide.
Front pair with flat tires	6¼ " "
Diameter of drivers	48 to 56 inches.

TRUCK.

FOUR WHEELED RADIATING TRUCK.

Diameter of wheels	24 to 28 inches.

WHEEL-BASE.

Total wheel-base	21 ft. 5 in. to 23 ft.
Distance between centres of front and rear drivers .	12 ft. to 13 ft. 6 inches.

TENDER.

ON EIGHT WHEELS.

Capacity of tank	2000 gallons.

WEIGHT OF ENGINE IN WORKING ORDER.

On drivers	54,830 lbs.
On truck	20,520 "
Total weight of engine about	75,350 lbs.

LOAD.

IN ADDITION TO ENGINE AND TENDER.

130 lbs. initial pressure, cylinders 18x22—56 inch wheel		Cyls. 18x24. 48 in. wheel.	
Admission	50%.	70%	50%.	70%.
On a level . . .	1485	1912	1899	2443
" 20 ft. grade .	686	891	880	1141
" 40 ' . .	433	568	557	728
" 60 " .	309	410	398	528
" 80 " .	236	316	304	407
' 100 " .	188	255	244	329

CLASS D. E.

LOCOMOTIVE ENGINES, FOR FREIGHT OR PASSENGER SERVICE.

GENERAL DESIGN ILLUSTRATED ON PAGE 101.

CYLINDERS.

Diameter of cylinders . . . . . . 11 inches.
Length of stroke . . . . 18 "

DRIVING-WHEELS.

Diameter of drivers . . . . . . 30¼ to 49 inches.

TRUCKS.

TWO WHEELED RADIATING TRUCK, FORWARD.

Diameter of wheels . . . . . . 24 to 30 inches.

TWO OR FOUR WHEELED TRUCK IN REAR WITH LATERAL MOTION.

Diameter of wheels . . . . . . 24 to 26 inches.

WHEEL-BASE.

Total wheel-base . . . . . 24 ft. 5 in. to 25 ft. 6 in.
Distance between centres of drivers, (4) . . 6 ft. 6 inches.

TANK.

PLACED UPON REAR END OF ENGINE FRAME.

Capacity of tank . . . . . . 400 to 1000 gallons.

WEIGHT OF ENGINE IN WORKING ORDER.

On drivers . . . . 31,000 lbs.
On front truck . . . . 7,100 "
On rear truck . . . . 25,500 "

Total weight of engine about . . . . 63,600 lbs.

LOAD.

IN ADDITION TO ENGINE AND TENDER.

130 lbs. initial pressure, cylinders 11x18—49 in. wheel		Cyls. 11x18. 30¼ in. wheel.	
Admission	50%.	70%.	50%.	70%.
On a level	479	631	822	1064
" 20 ft. grade	213	285	378	494
" 40 "	129	176	238	314
" 60 "	88	123	169	226
" 80 "	64	92	125	173
" 100 "	48	72	102	140

CLASS D. E.

LOCOMOTIVE ENGINES, FOR FREIGHT OR PASSENGER SERVICE.

GENERAL DESIGN ILLUSTRATED ON PAGE 101.

CYLINDERS.

Diameter of cylinders . . . . . . 12 inches.

Length of stroke . . . . 20 "

DRIVING-WHEELS.

Diameter of drivers . . . . . . 37 to 49 inches.

TRUCKS.

TWO WHEELED RADIATING TRUCK, FORWARD.

Diameter of wheels . . . . . . 26 to 30 inches.

TWO OR FOUR WHEELED TRUCK IN REAR, WITH LATERAL MOTION.

Diameter of wheels . . . . . . 24 to 26 inches.

WHEEL-BASE.

Total wheel-base . . . . . . 25 ft. to 25 ft. 6 inches.

Distance between centres of drivers, (4) . . 6 ft. 6 inches.

TANK.

PLACED UPON REAR END OF ENGINE FRAME.

Capacity of tank . . . . . . 400 to 1000 gallons.

WEIGHT OF ENGINE IN WORKING ORDER.

On drivers . . . . 33,000 lbs.

On front truck . . . . 7,200 "

On rear truck . . . . 25,300 "

Total weight of engine about . . . . 65,500 lbs.

LOAD.

IN ADDITION TO ENGINE AND TENDER.

130 lbs. initial pressure, cylinders 12x20—49 inch wheel		Cyls. 12x20. 37 in. wheel.	
Admission	50%.	70%	50%.	70%.
On a level	655	852	893	1154
" 20 ft. grade	297	392	411	537
" 40 "	184	246	259	342
" 60 "	129	175	185	246
" 80 "	96	133	140	190
" 100 "	75	106	112	153

CLASS D. E.

LOCOMOTIVE ENGINES, FOR FREIGHT OR PASSENGER SERVICE.

GENERAL DESIGN ILLUSTRATED ON PAGE 101.

CYLINDERS.

Diameter of cylinders . . . . . . 13 inches.
Length of stroke . . . . . . 20 or 22 "

DRIVING-WHEELS.

Diameter of drivers . . . . . . 37 to 49 inches.

TRUCKS.

TWO WHEELED RADIATING TRUCK, FORWARD.

Diameter of wheels . . . . . . 26 to 30 inches.

WHEEL-BASE.

Total wheel-base . . . . . 25 ft. 6 in. to 26 ft.
Distance between centres of drivers, (4) . . . . 6 ft. 6 inches.

TANK.

PLACED UPON REAR END OF ENGINE FRAME.

Capacity of tank . . . . . . 500 to 1000 gallons.

WEIGHT OF ENGINE IN WORKING ORDER.

On drivers . . . . 34,000 lbs.
On front truck . . . . . . 8,000 "
On rear truck . . . . 25,000 "
Total weight of engine about . . . . . 67,000 lbs.

LOAD.

IN ADDITION TO ENGINE AND TENDER.

130 lbs. initial pressure, cylinders 13x20—49 in. wheel		Cyls. 13x22.	37 in. wheel.	
Admission	50%.	70%.	50%.	70%.
On a level	777	1020	1166	1487
" 20 ft. grade	358	478	540	701
" 40 "	225	301	342	448
" 60 "	159	217	245	325
" 80 "	121	167	188	251
" 100 "	97	134	151	204

CLASS D. E.

LOCOMOTIVE ENGINES, FOR FREIGHT OR PASSENGER SERVICE.

GENERAL DESIGN ILLUSTRATED ON PAGE 106.

CYLINDERS.

Diameter of cylinders . . . . 14 inches.
Length of stroke . . . . . . 20 or 22 "

DRIVING-WHEELS.

Diameter of drivers . . . . . 37 to 49 inches.

TRUCKS.

TWO WHEELED RADIATING TRUCK, FORWARD.

Diameter of wheels . . . . . 26 to 30 inches.

TWO OR FOUR WHEELED TRUCK IN REAR, WITH LATERAL MOTION.

Diameter of wheels . . . . . 24 to 26 inches.

WHEEL-BASE.

Total wheel-base . . . . . 25 ft. 8 in. to 26 ft. 3 inches.
Distance between centres of drivers, (4) . 6 ft. 6 inches.

TANK.

PLACED UPON REAR END OF ENGINE FRAME.

Capacity of tank . . . . . . 500 to 1000 gallons.

WEIGHT OF ENGINE IN WORKING ORDER.

On drivers . . . . 36,000 lbs.
On front truck . . . . 9,000 "
On rear truck . . . . 25,000 "

Total weight of engine about . . . . 70,000 lbs.

LOAD.

IN ADDITION TO ENGINE AND TENDER.

130 lbs. initial pressure, cylinders 14x20—49 inch wheel		Cyls. 14x22. 37 in. wheel.	
Admission	50%.	70%	50%.	70%.
On a level	921	1199	1360	1752
" 20 ft. grade	426	555	633	821
" 40 "	269	354	403	526
" 60 "	192	256	290	382
" 80 "	147	198	223	297
" 100 "	118	159	180	242

CLASS D. E.

LOCOMOTIVE ENGINES, FOR FREIGHT OR PASSENGER SERVICE.

GENERAL DESIGN ILLUSTRATED ON PAGE 106.

CYLINDERS.

Diameter of cylinders	15 inches.
Length of stroke	20 or 22 "

DRIVING-WHEELS.

Diameter of drivers	37 to 49 inches.

TRUCKS.

TWO WHEELED RADIATING TRUCK, FORWARD.

Diameter of wheels	26 to 30 inches.

TWO OR FOUR WHEELED TRUCK IN REAR WITH LATERAL MOTION.

Diameter of wheels	24 to 26 inches

WHEEL-BASE.

Total wheel-base	26 ft. to 27 ft.
Distance between centres of drivers, (4)	6 ft. 6 inches.

TANK.

PLACED UPON REAR END OF ENGINE FRAME.

Capacity of tank	600 to 1200 gallons.

WEIGHT OF ENGINE IN WORKING ORDER.

On drivers	40,000 lbs.
On front truck	10,000 "
On rear truck	24,000 "
Total weight of engine about	74,000 lbs.

LOAD.

IN ADDITION TO ENGINE AND TENDER.

130 lbs. initial pressure, cylinders 15x20—49 in. wheel		Cyls. 15x22.	37 in. wheel.
Admission . 50%. . 70%.		50%. . .	70%.
On a level . . . 1064 . 1372		1570 . .	2019
" 20 ft. grade . 494 641		731 . .	948
" 40 " . . 313 . 410		467 . .	609
" 60 " . 224 . 297		336 . .	443
" 80 " . . 172 . 230		260 . .	345
" 100 " . 139 . 187		211 . .	281

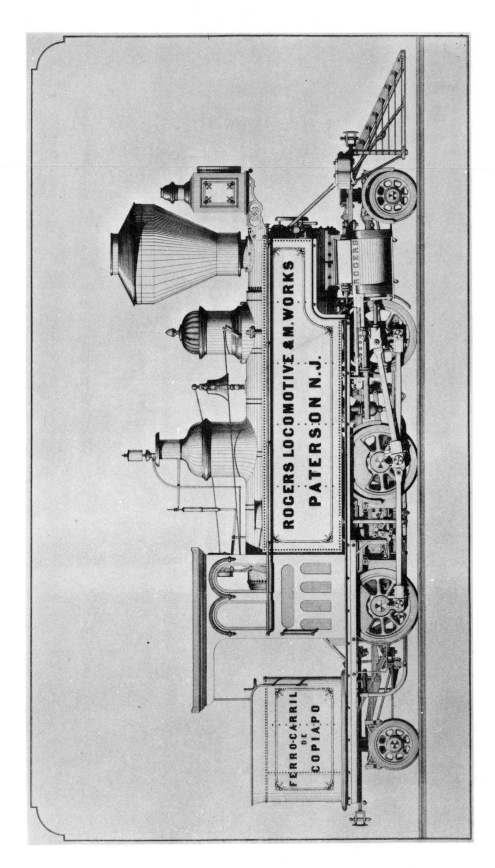

CLASS D. E.

LOCOMOTIVE ENGINES, FOR FREIGHT SERVICE.

GENERAL DESIGN ILLUSTRATED ON PAGE 110.

CYLINDERS.

Diameter of cylinders . . . . . . 15 inches.

Length of stroke . . . . . . 20 or 22 "

DRIVING-WHEELS.

Diameter of drivers . . . . . . 37 to 49 inches.

TRUCKS.

TWO WHEELED RADIATING TRUCK, FORWARD.

Diameter of wheels . . . . . 26 to 30 inches.

TWO WHEELED RADIATING TRUCK, IN REAR.

Diameter of wheels . . . . . 26 to 30 inches.

WHEEL-BASE.

Total wheel-base . . . . . 24 ft. to 25 ft.

Distance between centres of drivers, (6) . . 12 ft. to 12 ft. 6 inches.

TANK.

PLACED UPON REAR END OF ENGINE FRAME, AND ON EACH SIDE OF BOILER.

Capacity of tank . . . . . 1400 to 1600 gallons.

WEIGHT OF ENGINE IN WORKING ORDER.

On drivers . . . . 67,400 lbs.

On front truck . . . . 9,180 "

On rear truck . . . . 7,400 "

Total weight of engine about . . . . 83,980 lbs.

LOAD.

IN ADDITION TO ENGINE AND TENDER.

130 lbs. initial pressure, cylinders 15x20—49 inch wheel		Cyls. 15x22. 37 in. wheel.	
Admission	50%.	70%	50%.	70%.
On a level	1055	1362	1557	2007
" 20 ft. grade	487	634	723	939
" 40 "	307	404	459	601
" 60 "	219	291	331	436
" 80 "	167	225	254	338
" 100 "	133	181	204	275

CLASS M. T.

NARROW GAUGE LOCOMOTIVE ENGINES, FOR FREIGHT SERVICE.

GENERAL DESIGN ILLUSTRATED ON PAGE 113.

CYLINDERS.

Diameter of cylinders . . . . . .   10 inches.

Length of stroke . . . .   18 "

DRIVING-WHEELS.

REAR AND FRONT PAIRS WITH FLANGED TIRES 5¾ INCHES WIDE.

INTERMEDIATE PAIR WITH FLAT TIRES 6¼ INCHES WIDE.

Diameter of drivers, (6) . . . . . .   30 inches.

TRUCK.

SINGLE PAIR OF TRUCK WHEELS WITH LATERAL MOTION, AND CONNECTED BY EQUALIZING

LEVERS WITH FRONT DRIVERS.

Diameter of wheels . . . .   20 inches.

WHEEL-BASE.

Total wheel-base . . . . . .   13 ft. 10 inches.

Rigid wheel-base, distance between centres of front and rear drivers, (6)   9 feet.

TANK.

Capacity of tank . . . . . .   300 to 450 gallons.

WEIGHT OF ENGINE IN WORKING ORDER.

On drivers . . . .   26,000 lbs.

On truck . . . .   6,000 "

Total weight of engine about . . . . .   32,000 lbs.

LOAD.

IN ADDITION TO ENGINE AND TENDER.

130 lbs. initial pressure, cylinders 10x18—30 in. wheel.

	Admission	50%.	70%.
On a level		709	910
" 20 ft. grade		332	428
" 40 "		213	276
" 60 "		154	202
" 80 "		120	157
" 100 "		96	128

CLASS M. T.

NARROW GAUGE LOCOMOTIVE ENGINE, FOR FREIGHT SERVICE.

GENERAL DESIGN ILLUSTRATED ON PAGE 113.

CYLINDERS.

Diameter of cylinders	11 inches.
Length of stroke	18 "

DRIVING-WHEELS.

REAR AND FRONT PAIRS WITH FLANGED TIRES 5¾ INCHES WIDE.
INTERMEDIATE PAIR WITH FLAT TIRES 6¼ INCHES WIDE.

Diameter of drivers, (6)	30 inches.

TRUCK.

SINGLE PAIR OF TRUCK WHEELS WITH LATERAL MOTION, AND CONNECTED BY EQUALIZING
LEVERS WITH FRONT DRIVERS.

Diameter of wheels	20 inches.

WHEEL-BASE.

Total wheel-base	13 ft. 10 inches.
Rigid wheel-base, distance between centres of front and rear drivers, (6)	9 feet.

TANK.

Capacity of tank	400 to 500 gallons.

WEIGHT OF ENGINE IN WORKING ORDER.

On drivers	31,000 lbs.
On truck	7,000 "
Total weight of engine about	38,000 lbs.

LOAD.

IN ADDITION TO ENGINE AND TENDER.

130 lbs. initial pressure, cylinders 11x18—30 in. wheel.

	Admission 50%.	70%.
On a level	859	1102
" 20 ft. grade	402	519
" 40 "	258	335
" 60 "	187	245
" 80 "	145	191
" 100 "	118	157

CLASS M. T.

NARROW GAUGE LOCOMOTIVE ENGINE, FOR FREIGHT SERVICE.

GENERAL DESIGN ILLUSTRATED ON PAGE 113.

CYLINDERS.

Diameter of cylinders . . . . . .   12 inches.
Length of stroke   18   "

DRIVING-WHEELS.

REAR AND FRONT PAIRS WITH FLANGED TIRES 5¾ INCHES WIDE.
INTERMEDIATE PAIR WITH FLAT TIRES 6¼ INCHES WIDE.

Diameter of drivers . . . .   30 inches.

TRUCK.

SINGLE PAIR OF TRUCK WHEELS WITH LATERAL MOTION, AND CONNECTED BY EQUALIZING
LEVER WITH FRONT DRIVERS.

Diameter of wheels . . . .   20 inches.

WHEEL-BASE.

Total wheel-base . . . . . .   13 ft. 10 inches.
Rigid wheel-base, distance between centres of front and rear drivers, (6)   9 feet.

TANK.

Capacity of tank . . . .   500 gallons.

WEIGHT OF ENGINE IN WORKING ORDER.

On drivers . . . .   35,000 lbs.
On truck   7,000   "
Total weight of engine about . . . . .   42,000 lbs.

LOAD.

IN ADDITION TO ENGINE AND TENDER.

130 lbs. initial pressure, cylinders 12x18—30 in. wheel.

	Admission	50%.				70%.
On a level		1025				1316
" 20 ft. grade		481				621
" 40 "		309				401
" 60 "		225				293
" 80 "		175				229
" 100 "		143				188

CLASS M. T.

NARROW GAUGE LOCOMOTIVE ENGINE, FOR FREIGHT SERVICE.

GENERAL DESIGN ILLUSTRATED ON PAGE 113.

CYLINDERS.

Diameter of cylinders	13 inches.
Length of stroke	18 "

DRIVING-WHEELS.

REAR AND FRONT PAIRS WITH FLANGED TIRES 5¾ INCHES WIDE.
INTERMEDIATE PAIR WITH FLAT TIRES 6¼ INCHES WIDE.

Diameter of drivers	30 inches.

TRUCK.

SINGLE PAIR OF TRUCK WHEELS WITH LATERAL MOTION, AND CONNECTED BY EQUALIZING
LEVERS WITH FRONT DRIVERS.

Diameter of wheels	20 inches.

WHEEL-BASE.

Total wheel-base	13 ft. 10 inches.
Rigid wheel-base, distance between centres of front and rear drivers, (6)	9 feet.

TANK.

Capacity of tank	600 gallons.

WEIGHT OF ENGINE IN WORKING ORDER.

On drivers	38,770 lbs.
On truck	7,840 "
Total weight of engine about	46,610 lbs.

LOAD.

IN ADDITION TO ENGINE AND TENDER.

130 lbs. initial pressure, cylinders 13x18—30 in. wheel.

	Admission	50%.	70%.
On a level		1206	1547
" 20 ft. grade		567	731
" 40 "		365	472
" 60 "		266	346
" 80 "		207	271
" 100 "		170	222

CLASS M. TEN.

NARROW GAUGE LOCOMOTIVE ENGINES, FOR FREIGHT SERVICE.

GENERAL DESIGN ILLUSTRATED ON PAGE 119.

CYLINDERS.

Diameter of cylinders . . . . 13 inches.
Length of stroke . . . . 18 "

DRIVING-WHEELS.

REAR AND FRONT PAIRS WITH FLANGED TIRES 5¾ INCHES WIDE.
INTERMEDIATE PAIR WITH FLAT TIRES 6¼ INCHES WIDE.

Diameter of drivers . . . . . . 30 to 37 inches.

TRUCKS.

TWO WHEELED RADIATING TRUCK, FORWARD.

Diameter of wheels . . . . 24 inches.

EIGHT WHEELED TENDER, FRONT TENDER TRUCK WITH LATERAL MOTION, AND EXCESS OF WEIGHT OF REAR END OF ENGINE SUPPORTED BY FRONT END OF TENDER.

Diameter of wheels . . . . 24 inches.

WHEEL-BASE.

Total wheel-base (including tender) . 33 ft. 3 in. to 33 ft. 9 inches.
Rigid " . . . . . 7 ft. 6 inches.

TANK.

Capacity of tank . . . . 1000 gallons.

WEIGHT OF ENGINE IN WORKING ORDER (including Tender).

On drivers . . . . 34,000 lbs.
On leading wheels . . . . . . 6,000 "
On forward tender truck ⎫
On back " " ⎭ . . . . . 26,000 "

Total weight of engine (including tender) . . . . 66,000 lbs.

LOAD.

IN ADDITION TO ENGINE AND TENDER.

130 lbs. initial pressure, cylinders 13x18—37 inch wheel			Cyls. 13x18.		30 in. wheel.
Admission .	50%.	70%	50%. .	.	70%.
On a level . . .	960 .	. 1235	1198	.	. 1538
" 20 ft. grade	443	576	558	.	721
" 40 " .	280 .	. 367	355	.	463
" 60 " .	201	. 266	257	.	337
" 80 " .	153 .	205	197	.	261
" 100 " .	122	. 165	159	.	213

CLASS M. TEN.

NARROW GAUGE LOCOMOTIVE ENGINES, FOR FREIGHT SERVICE.

GENERAL DESIGN ILLUSTRATED ON PAGE 119.

CYLINDERS.

Diameter of cylinders . . . . 14 inches.
Length of stroke . . . . . . 18 "

DRIVING-WHEELS.

REAR AND FRONT PAIRS WITH FLANGED TIRES 5¾ INCHES WIDE.
INTERMEDIATE PAIR WITH FLAT TIRES 6¼ INCHES WIDE.

Diameter of drivers . . . . . . 30 to 37 inches.

TRUCKS.

TWO WHEELED RADIATING TRUCK, FORWARD.

Diameter of wheels . . . . 24 inches.

EIGHT WHEELED TENDER, FRONT TRUCK WITH LATERAL MOTION, AND EXCESS OF WEIGHT
OF REAR END OF ENGINE SUPPORTED BY FRONT END OF TENDER.

Diameter of wheels . . . . . . 24 inches.

WHEEL-BASE.

Total wheel-base (including tender) . . 33 ft. 3 in. to 33 ft. 9 inches.
Rigid " . . . . . 7 ft. 6 inches.

TANK.

Capacity of tank . . . . 1200 gallons.

WEIGHT OF ENGINE IN WORKING ORDER (including Tender).

On drivers . . . . 40,000 lbs.
On leading wheels . . . . 8,000 "
On forward tender truck }
On back " " } . . . . . 28,000 "

———
Total weight of engine (including tender) . . . . 76,000 lbs.

LOAD.

IN ADDITION TO ENGINE AND TENDER.

130 lbs. initial pressure, cylinders 14x18—37 inch wheel			Cyls. 14x18.	30 in. wheel.	
Admission	50%.	70%	50%.		70%.
On a level	1112	1433	1388		1784
" 20 ft. grade	514	668	646		837
" 40 "	325	426	412		537
" 60 "	232	308	297		390
" 80 "	177	238	229		303
" 100 "	142	193	185		247

CLASS M. TEN.

NARROW GAUGE LOCOMOTIVE ENGINES, FOR FREIGHT SERVICE.

GENERAL DESIGN ILLUSTRATED ON PAGE 119.

CYLINDERS.

Diameter of cylinders . . . . 15 inches.
Length of stroke . . . . 18 "

DRIVING-WHEELS.

REAR AND FRONT PAIRS WITH FLANGED TIRES 5¾ INCHES WIDE.
INTERMEDIATE PAIR WITH FLAT TIRES 6¼ INCHES WIDE.

Diameter of drivers . . . . . 30 to 37 inches.

TRUCKS.

TWO WHEELED RADIATING TRUCK, FORWARD.

Diameter of wheels . . . . 24 inches.

EIGHT WHEELED TENDER, FRONT TRUCK WITH LATERAL MOTION, AND EXCESS OF WEIGHT
OF REAR END OF ENGINE SUPPORTED BY FRONT END OF TENDER.

WHEEL-BASE.

Total wheel-base (including tender) . . 33 ft. 3 in. to 33 ft. 9 inches.
Rigid   " . . . . . 7 ft. 6 inches.

TANK.

Capacity of tank . . . . 1200 gallons.

WEIGHT OF ENGINE IN WORKING ORDER (including Tender).

On drivers . . . . 43,000 lbs.
On leading wheels . . . . . . 8,000 "
On forward tender truck ⎫
On back   "   "   ⎭ . . . . . 30,000 "
                                                    ————
Total weight of engine (including tender) . . . . 81,000 lbs.

LOAD.

IN ADDITION TO ENGINE AND TENDER.

130 lbs. initial pressure, cylinders 15x18—37 inch wheel		Cyls. 15x18. 30 in. wheel.	
Admission	50%.	70%	50%.	70%.

	50%	70%	50%	70%
Admission	50%.	70%	50%.	70%.
On a level	1283	1650	1600	2053
" 20 ft. grade	588	771	747	965
" 40 "	377	493	478	621
" 60 "	271	357	345	452
" 80 "	207	276	269	352
" 100 "	166	224	216	287

124

CLASS S. T.

NARROW GAUGE SWITCHING TANK ENGINE.

GENERAL DESIGN ILLUSTRATED ON PAGE 124.

CYLINDERS.

Diameter of cylinders	8 inches.
Length of stroke	12 inches.

DRIVING WHEELS.

Diameter of drivers	26 to 30 inches.
Distance between centres	5 feet.

TANK.

Capacity	175 gallons.

WEIGHT OF ENGINE IN WORKING ORDER.

Total weight of engine about	18,500 lbs.

LOAD.

IN ADDITION TO ENGINE AND TENDER.

130 lbs. initial pressure, cylinders 8x12—30 inch wheel. |Cyls. 8x12. 26 in. wheel.

	Admission 50%.	70%.	50%.	70%.
On a level . . .	297 .	383	346 . .	445
" 20 ft. grade .	137 .	172	161 . .	209
" 40 " . .	87 .	114	102 . .	134
" 60 " . .	62 .	83	74 . .	97
" 80 " . .	48 .	64	57 . .	76
" 100 " . .	39 .	52	46 . .	62

CLASS S. T.

NARROW GAUGE SWITCHING TANK ENGINE.

GENERAL DESIGN ILLUSTRATED ON PAGE 124.

CYLINDERS.

Diameter of cylinders	9 inches.
Length of stroke	12 inches.

DRIVING WHEELS.

Diameter of drivers	26 to 33 inches.
Distance between centres	5 feet.

TANK.

Capacity	200 gallons.

WEIGHT OF ENGINE IN WORKING ORDER.

Total weight of engine about	21,700 lbs.

LOAD.

IN ADDITION TO ENGINE AND TENDER.

130 lbs. initial pressure, cylinders 9x12—33 inch wheel.		Cyls. 9x12. 26 in. wheel.	
Admission	50%.	70%.	50%.	70%.
On a level	341	440	440	565
" 20 ft. grade	158	205	205	265
" 40 "	100	131	131	171
" 60 "	71	95	95	124
" 80 "	55	73	73	97
" 100 "	44	59	60	79

CLASS S. T.

NARROW GAUGE SWITCHING TANK ENGINE.

GENERAL DESIGN ILLUSTRATED ON PAGE 124.

CYLINDERS.

Diameter of cylinders . . . . 10 inches.
Length of stroke . . . . 12 inches.

DRIVING WHEELS.

Diameter of drivers . . . . . . 26 to 36 inches.
Distance between centres . . . . . . 5 feet.

TANK.

Capacity . . . . 225 gallons.

WEIGHT OF ENGINE IN WORKING ORDER.

Total weight of engine about . . . . . 23,000 lbs.

LOAD.

IN ADDITION TO ENGINE AND TENDER.

130 lbs. initial pressure, cylinders 10x12—36 inch wheel.		Cyls. 10x12. 26 in. wheel.	
Admission 50%.	70%.	50%.	70%.
On a level . . . 402 . . 500		547 . .	702
" 20 ft. grade . 180 . . 234		256 .	331
" 40 " . . 114 . . 150		165 . .	214
" 60 " . . 82 . 109		120 . .	156
" 80 " . . 63 . . 84		93 . . .	122
" 100 " . . 51 . 69		76 . .	100

CLASS S.

NARROW GAUGE SWITCHING ENGINE, WITH SEPARATE TENDER.

GENERAL DESIGN ILLUSTRATED ON PAGE 129.

CYLINDERS.

Diameter of cylinders	9 inches.
Length of stroke	12 inches.

DRIVING WHEELS.

Diameter of drivers	26 to 30 inches
Distance between centres	7 ft. 10 to 8 ft. 4 inches.

TENDER.

ON FOUR TO EIGHT WHEELS.

Capacity of tank	500 to 1000 gallons.

WEIGHT OF ENGINE IN WORKING ORDER.

Total weight of engine about	20,000 lbs.

LOAD.

IN ADDITION TO ENGINE AND TENDER.

130 lbs. initial pressure, cylinders 9x12—30 inch wheel.		Cyls. 9x12.	26 in. wheel.	
Admission	50%.	70%.	50%.	70%.
On a level	372	481	434	559
" 20 ft. grade	169	221	199	259
" 40 "	105	139	124	164
" 60 "	73	99	88	118
" 80 "	55	75	66	90
" 100 "	43	60	53	72

CLASS S.

NARROW GAUGE SWITCHING ENGINES, WITH SEPARATE TENDER.

GENERAL DESIGN ILLUSTRATED ON PAGE 129.

CYLINDERS.

Diameter of cylinders . . . . . . 10 inches.

Length of stroke . . . . 14 inches.

DRIVING WHEELS.

Diameter of drivers . . . . . . 28 to 33 inches.

Distance between centres . . . . 8 ft. to 8 ft. 8 inches.

TENDER.

ON FOUR TO EIGHT WHEELS.

Capacity of tank . . . . . . 600 to 1000 gallons.

WEIGHT OF ENGINE IN WORKING ORDER.

Total weight of engine about . . . . . 21,000 lbs.

LOAD.

IN ADDITION TO ENGINE AND TENDER.

130 lbs. initial pressure, cylinders 10x14—33 inch wheel.		Cyls. 10x14. 28 in. wheel.	
Admission . 50%. . 70%.		50%. . 70%.	
On a level . . . 495 . . 638		575 . . 757	
" 20 ft. grade 228 . 296		273 . . 354	
" 40 " . . 143 . . 189		173 . . 226	
" 60 " . . 102 . 136		124 . . 164	
" 80 " . . 77 . . 104		95 . . 127	
" 00 " . . 62 . 84		77 . . 103	

CLASS S.

NARROW GAUGE SWITCHING ENGINES, WITH SEPARATE TENDER.

GENERAL DESIGN ILLUSTRATED ON PAGE 129.

CYLINDERS.

Diameter of cylinders . . . . . . 12 inches.
Length of stroke . . . . 16 inches.

DRIVING WHEELS.

Diameter of drivers . . . . . . 30 to 36 inches.
Distance between centres . . . . 8 ft. 4 in. to 9 feet.

TENDER.

ON FOUR TO EIGHT WHEELS.

Capacity of tank . . . . . . 600 to 1200 gallons.

WEIGHT OF ENGINE IN WORKING ORDER.

Total weight of engine about . . . . . 22,000 lbs.

LOAD.

IN ADDITION TO ENGINE AND TENDER.

130 lbs. initial pressure, cylinders 12x16—36 inch wheel.		Cyls. 12x16. 30 in. wheel.	
Admission . 50%. . 70%.		50%. . . 70%.	
On a level . . . 762 . . 974		920 . . 1178	
" 20 ft. grade . 355 . 457		431 . . 555	
" 40 " . . 227 . . 294		277 . . 358	
" 60 " . . 164 . . 214		201 . . 262	
" 80 " . 126 . . 166		156 . . 204	
" 100 " . . 103 . 136		127 . . 168	

CLASS D. E.

NARROW GAUGE LOCOMOTIVE ENGINES, FOR FREIGHT OR PASSENGER SERVICE.

GENERAL DESIGN ILLUSTRATED ON PAGE 134.

CYLINDERS.

Diameter of cylinders	9 inches.
Length of stroke	12 "

DRIVING-WHEELS.

Diameter of drivers	30 to 36 inches.

TRUCKS.
TWO WHEELED RADIATING TRUCK, FORWARD.

Diameter of wheels	24 to 26 inches.

TWO OR FOUR WHEELED TRUCK IN REAR WITH LATERAL MOTION.

Diameter of wheels	24 to 26 inches.

WHEEL-BASE.

Total wheel-base	22 ft. to 23 ft. 6 inches.
Distance between centres of drivers	6 feet.

TANK.
PLACED UPON REAR END OF ENGINE FRAME.

Capacity of tank	250 to 600 gallons.

WEIGHT OF ENGINE IN WORKING ORDER.

On drivers	20,000 lbs.
On front truck	5,000 "
On rear truck	14,000 "
Total weight of engine about	39,000 lbs.

LOAD.
IN ADDITION TO ENGINE.

130 lbs. initial pressure, cylinders 9x12—36 inch wheel		Cyls. 9x12. 30 in. wheel.	
Admission	50%. 70%	50%.	70%.
On a level	291 382	358	467
" 20 ft. grade	129 173	161	214
" 40 "	78 107	99	134
" 60 "	53 75	69	95
" 80 "	38 55	51	71
" 100 "	29 43	39	56

CLASS D. E.

NARROW GAUGE LOCOMOTIVE ENGINES, FOR FREIGHT OR PASSENGER SERVICE.

GENERAL DESIGN ILLUSTRATED ON PAGE 134.

CYLINDERS.

Diameter of cylinders	10 inches.
Length of stroke	16 "

DRIVING-WHEELS.

Diameter of drivers	30 to 36 inches.

TRUCKS.
TWO WHEELED RADIATING TRUCK, FORWARD.

Diameter of wheels	24 to 26 inches.

TWO OR FOUR WHEELED TRUCK IN REAR WITH LATERAL MOTION.

Diameter of wheels	24 to 26 inches.

WHEEL-BASE.

Total wheel-base	23 ft. to 24 ft. 6 inches.
Distance between centres of drivers	6 feet.

TANK.
PLACED UPON REAR END OF ENGINE FRAME.

Capacity of tank	250 to 600 gallons.

WEIGHT OF ENGINE IN WORKING ORDER.

On drivers	22,000 lbs.
On front truck	5,500 "
On rear truck	15,000 "
Total weight of engine about	42,500 lbs.

LOAD.
IN ADDITION TO ENGINE.

130 lbs. initial pressure, cylinders 10x16—36 in. wheel.		Cyls. 10x16.	30 in. wheel.	
Admission	50%.	70%.	50%.	70%.
On a level	504	653	614	793
" 20 ft. grade	231	302	284	370
" 40 "	149	192	179	236
" 60 "	102	137	128	170
" 80 "	77	105	98	131
" 100 "	61	84	78	106

CLASS D. E.

NARROW GAUGE LOCOMOTIVE ENGINES, FOR FREIGHT OR PASSENGER SERVICE.

GENERAL DESIGN ILLUSTRATED ON PAGE 134.

CYLINDERS.

Diameter of cylinders	11 inches.
Length of stroke	16 "

DRIVING-WHEELS.

Diameter of drivers	30 to 36 inches.

TRUCKS.

TWO WHEELED RADIATING TRUCK, FORWARD.

Diameter of wheels	24 to 26 inches.

TWO OR FOUR WHEELED TRUCK IN REAR WITH LATERAL MOTION.

Diameter of wheels	24 to 26 inches.

WHEEL-BASE.

Total wheel-base	23 ft. to 24 ft. 6 inches.
Distance between centres of drivers . .	6 feet.

TANK.

PLACED UPON REAR END OF ENGINE FRAME.

Capacity of tank	250 to 600 gallons.

WEIGHT OF ENGINE IN WORKING ORDER.

On drivers	23,000 lbs.
On front truck	6,000 "
On rear truck	16,000 "
Total weight of engine about	45,000 lbs.

LOAD.

IN ADDITION TO ENGINE.

130 lbs. initial pressure, cylinders 11x16—36 inch wheel | Cyls. 11x16. 30 in. wheel.

	50%.	70%	50%.	70%.
Admission				
On a level . .	617 .	. 798	750 .	. 967
" 20 ft. grade .	284 .	. 371	349 .	. 453
" 40 " .	179 .	. 236	221	. 290
" 60 " .	128 .	. 170	159 .	. 210
" 80 " .	97 .	. 131	122	. 162
" 100 " .	76 .	. 106	98 .	. 132

CLASS I. E.

ORDINARY AND NARROW GAUGE LOCOMOTIVE ENGINES, FOR INSPECTORS' USE.

GENERAL DESIGN ILLUSTRATED ON PAGE 139.

CYLINDERS.

Diameter of cylinders	4 in. or 5 inches.
Length of stroke	12 inches.

DRIVING WHEELS.

Diameter of drivers	28 to 30 inches.

CARRYING WHEELS.

Diameter of wheels	28 to 30 inches.
Distance between centres . . .	7 ft. 3 in. to 7 ft. 6 inches.

TANKS.

Capacity	120 to 140 gallons.

WEIGHT OF ENGINE IN WORKING ORDER.

Total weight of engine about . . .	8,500 to 13,500 lbs.

LOAD.

IN ADDITION TO ENGINE AND TENDER.

130 lbs. initial pressure, cylinders 4x12—30 inch wheel.		Cyls. 5x12. 28 in. whee..	
Admission	50%.	70%.	50%.	70%.
On a level . . .	68	91	116	152
" 20 ft. grade .	29	41	52	70
" 40 " . .	17	24	32	43
" 60 " . .	11	16	22	31
" 80 " . .	7	11	16	23
" 100 " . .	5	9	13	18

CLASSES F. T. & P. T.

TANK LOCOMOTIVE ENGINES, FOR FREIGHT OR PASSENGER SERVICE.

GENERAL DESIGN ILLUSTRATED ON PAGE 142.

CYLINDERS.

Diameter of cylinders	10 inches.
Length of stroke	18 inches.

DRIVING WHEELS.

Diameter of drivers	45 to 56 inches.
Distance between centres	6 ft. 6 inches.

TRUCK.
FOUR WHEELED CENTRE BEARING TRUCK.

Diameter of wheels	20 to 26 inches.

WHEEL-BASE.

Total wheel-base	16 ft. 11 inches.

TANK.

Capacity of tank	350 to 450 gallons.

WEIGHT OF ENGINE IN WORKING ORDER.

On drivers	20,000 lbs.
On truck	14,000 "
Total weight of engine about	34,000 lbs.

LOAD.
IN ADDITION TO ENGINE AND TENDER.

130 lbs. initial pressure, cylinders 10x18—56 inch wheel.		Cyls. 10x18. 45 in. wheel.	
Admission	50%.	70%.	50%.	70%.
On a level	360	468	458	592
" 20 ft. grade	164	215	211	275
" 40 "	102	136	133	175
" 60 "	71	97	94	126
" 80 "	53	74	70	97
" 100 "	42	60	57	78

CLASSES F. T. & P. T.

TANK LOCOMOTIVE ENGINES, FOR FREIGHT OR PASSENGER SERVICE.

GENERAL DESIGN ILLUSTRATED ON PAGE 142.

CYLINDERS.

Diameter of cylinders	11 inches.
Length of stroke	18 or 20 inches.

DRIVING WHEELS.

Diameter of drivers	45 to 56 inches.
Distance between centres	6 ft. 6 inches.

TRUCK.

FOUR WHEELED CENTRE BEARING TRUCK.

Diameter of wheels	20 to 26 inches.

WHEEL-BASE.

Total wheel-base	17 ft. 2 inches.

TANK.

Capacity of tank	400 to 500 gallons.

WEIGHT OF ENGINE IN WORKING ORDER.

On drivers	24,000 lbs.
On truck	16,000 "
Total weight of engine about	40,000 lbs.

LOAD.

IN ADDITION TO ENGINE AND TENDER.

130 lbs. initial pressure, cylinders 11x18—56 inch wheel. | Cyls. 11x20. 45 in. wheel.

	Admission	50%.	70%.	50%.	70%.
On a level		442	573	617	800
" 20 ft. grade		203	266	284	371
" 40 "		127	169	180	236
" 60 "		90	121	127	171
" 80 "		68	93	97	131
" 100 "		54	75	77	106

CLASSES F. T. & P. T.

TANK LOCOMOTIVE ENGINES, FOR FREIGHT OR PASSENGER SERVICE.

GENERAL DESIGN ILLUSTRATED ON PAGE 142.

CYLINDERS.

Diameter of cylinders . . . . . . 12 inches.
Length of stroke . . . . 18 or 20 inches.

DRIVING WHEELS.

Diameter of drivers . . . . . . 45 to 56 inches.
Distance between centres . . . . . 6 ft. 9 inches.

TRUCK.

FOUR WHEELED CENTRE BEARING TRUCK.

Diameter of wheels . . . . . . 20 to 26 inches.

WHEEL-BASE.

Total wheel-base . . . . . . 17 ft. 6 inches.

TANK.

Capacity of tank . . . . . . 450 to 550 gallons.

WEIGHT OF ENGINE IN WORKING ORDER.

On drivers . . . . 27,000 lbs.
On truck . . , ... 17,000 "
Total weight of engine about . . . . . 44,000 lbs.

LOAD.

IN ADDITION TO ENGINE AND TENDER.

130 lbs. initial pressure, cylinders 12x18—56 inch wheel.		Cyls. 12x20. 45 in. wheel.	
Admission 50%.	70%.	50%.	70%.
On a level . . 517	685	740 . .	955
" 20 ft. grade . 244	319	342 .	445
" 40 " . . 153	203	216 . .	284
" 60 " . 109	146	155 . .	205
" 80 " . . 83	112	119 .	159
" 100 " . 67	91	95 . .	129

CLASS P. T.

TANK LOCOMOTIVE ENGINES, FOR PASSENGER SERVICE.

GENERAL DESIGN ILLUSTRATED ON PAGE 147.

CYLINDERS.

Diameter of cylinders . . . . . .   8 inches.

Length of stroke . . . .   12 inches.

DRIVING WHEELS.

Diameter of drivers . . . . .   38 to 42 inches.

TRUCK.

FOUR WHEELED CENTRE BEARING TRUCK.

Diameter of wheels . . . . . .   20 to 24 inches.

WHEEL-BASE.

Total wheel-base . . . .   12 feet,

TANK.

Capacity . . . .   450 gallons.

WEIGHT OF ENGINE IN WORKING ORDER.

On drivers . . . .   19,039 lbs.

On truck . . . .   10,044 "

Total weight of engine about . . . .   29,083 lbs.

LOAD.

IN ADDITION TO ENGINE AND TENDER.

130 lbs. initial pressure, cylinders 8x12—42 inch wheel.		Cyls. 8x12. 38 in. wheel.	
Admission	50%.	70%.	50%.	70%.
On a level	194	255	218	286
" 20 ft. grade	85	115	97	129
" 40 "	51	70	59	80
" 60 "	34	49	40	56
" 80 "	24	36	29	41
" 100 "	18	28	22	33

CLASS P. T.

TANK LOCOMOTIVE ENGINES, FOR PASSENGER SERVICE.

GENERAL DESIGN ILLUSTRATED ON PAGE 147.

CYLINDERS.

Diameter of cylinders . . . . . . 9 inches.
Length of stroke . . . . 12 inches.

DRIVING WHEELS.

Diameter of drivers . . . . . . 38 to 42 inches.

TRUCK.

FOUR WHEELED CENTRE BEARING TRUCK.

Diameter of wheels . . . . . . 20 to 24 inches.

WHEEL-BASE.

Total wheel-base . . . . 12 feet,

TANK.

Capacity . . . . 500 gallons.

WEIGHT OF ENGINE IN WORKING ORDER.

On drivers . . . . 21,000 lbs.
On truck . . . . 11,000 "
Total weight of engine about . . . . 32,000 lbs.

LOAD.

IN ADDITION TO ENGINE AND TENDER.

130 lbs. initial pressure, cylinders 9x12—42 inch wheel.			Cyls. 9x12.	38 in. wheel.	
Admission	50%.	70%.	50%.		70%.
On a level	251	329	282		367
" 20 ft. grade	112	149	126		168
" 40 "	68	92	78		105
" 60 "	46	65	54		74
" 80 "	34	48	39		55
" 100 "	25	37	30		43